MW01068120

DIVINE COMPANY

BRILLIANT GODS
The Wisdom of Olympus
Book One

DIVINE
COMPANY

Invitations

F. T. Kettering

Copyright © 2009 by Frederick Thomas Kettering

All rights reserved, including the right of reproduction
or transmission in whole or in part in any form

Cover design by the author

ISBN 1442163569
EAN 9781442163560

Printed in the United States of America

for Alison,
who meets me in the stone circle

CONTENTS

Introduction   *xi*

Prologue   *xv*

A   **Shaping Gods**   1

B   **Breaking Free**   7

Γ   **Classic Advice**   11

Δ   **Shaping Greeks**   17

E   **Divine Company: At Home**   29

Z   **Divine Company: At Work**   33

H   **Divine Company: On the Land**   37

Θ   **Divine Company: On the Sea**   41

I   Divine Company: In Love   45

K   Divine Company: At War   49

Λ   Divine Company: In the City   53

M   Divine Company: On the Road   57

N   Divine Company: In Nature   61

Ξ   Divine Company: In Culture   67

O   Divine Company: In Each Other   71

Π   Divine Company: In the Cosmos   77

P   The Twelve   83

Σ   Family Traits   91

T   Standing Outside   97

Υ   After Life   103

Φ   One Answer   109

X   Multiple Choice   117

Ψ   Shaping Us   127

Ω   Shaping Up   137

Introduction

Imagine two paintings of a willow by a lake. One painting renders every leaf, every ripple of water with photographic clarity. The other captures the play of light in loose brushstrokes and bright splashes of color. Nobody would say that one image is true and the other false. Works of art do not contradict each other. Each of the paintings shows us something that the other does not show. Neither of them alters the physical reality of the tree or the lake.

Twenty-five centuries ago, a Greek poet sang to Zeus: "In you we live and move and have our being." A playwright wrote: "Zeus is earth, Zeus is sky, Zeus is everything, and more than that." Educated Greeks revered Zeus as the universal god who contains all of nature. Yet they also knew him as one of the twelve Olympians, the beautiful gods and goddesses who resemble human beings.

How could the ancient Greeks worship a singular divine and a plural divine at the same time? Their gods had made themselves known through myth. Like works of art, myths do not contradict each other. One myth tells us things that another does not tell. Equally important, the sort of knowledge provided by myth does not contradict the sort of knowledge provided by science.

For two millennia most people in the West have shared a single construct of what religion means. It involves a set of beliefs and a set of rituals, both of them grounded in scripture. Today, whether you embrace or reject ideas about "God," your ideas about "religion" are likely to conform to this model.

The Greeks developed an entirely different model, approaching the sacred in an entirely different way. They had little interest in faith and even less interest in scripture. Recognizing the spiritual value of myth and metaphor, they chose imagination over dogma.

BRILLIANT GODS: The Wisdom of Olympus is an integrated cycle of five books about the Greek deities. Only a fraction of this material deals with the past. With good reason these gods and goddesses are called "immortals." Paying close attention to them today will not turn us into ancient Greeks, but it may help us heal the rift between what we believe and what we know.

Book One
Divine Company
Invitations

Book Two
The Stones of Hermes
Explorations

Book Three
Labyrinth and Moon
Initiations

Book Four
The Hours of Aphrodite
Celebrations

Book Five
Oracle and Sun
Inspirations

The first book, **Divine Company**, discusses the past and present relevance of the gods. It has three main themes:

1) The world we imagine shapes the world we inhabit.
2) The vivid gods and goddesses of Olympus made the Greek achievement possible.
3) A sensible religion improves human life.

The other four volumes are fictions—moral tales. All are set in Northern California. *The Stones of Hermes* recounts the visit of two ships to the port of Monterey in 1786. French sailors and scientists befriend Spanish soldiers and missionaries. More surprisingly, they befriend Indians. *Labyrinth and Moon* takes place in present-day Santa Cruz. A student majoring in ecology runs into a smart, lively teen who calls herself Artemis; he learns a great deal. Like a medieval book of hours, *The Hours of Aphrodite* is a kind of prayer book, though its illustrations are musical rather than visual. It follows a dancer, a Berkeley undergrad, through her richly erotic day. The last volume, *Oracle and Sun*, is set in the near future on the flank of Mount Tamalpais. The Sanctuary of Apollo celebrates its twelfth year.

While these five books may be read in any sequence, the suggested order offers a logical progression from discovery to full engagement. *Divine Company* invites the reader to consider religion in a radically new light. *The Stones of Hermes* explores several monotheistic traditions from a polytheist's perspective. *Labyrinth and Moon* describes two rites of passage, one ancient and one modern. *The Hours of Aphrodite* watches a devotee enjoying the gifts of her favorite goddess. *Oracle and Sun* builds a temple for a wise young god.

Prologue

The sky was white, the earth yellow with heat.
We had seen no rain for weeks.

Shortly after sunset a light breeze came down
off the mountain. Then the first drops fell.
The rain continued through the night,
gentle but steady, ending just as the sun rose.
We awoke to birdsong and the smell of wet
leaves. Early risers went outside to enjoy the
cool, fresh morning.

When we met our neighbors, they seemed
changed. People we had known for years looked
new to us, and somehow splendid. We said,
"Good morning." They said, "Good morning."
It sounded like music. We stopped to talk.

For as long as anyone could remember, we had
asked each other the same question: "What do
you believe?" And now—suddenly—we found
ourselves asking, "What do you imagine?"

SHAPING GODS

If you are human, you are a god-shaper. You can't help it. But you *can* help it along.

If you are human, you are a god-shaper. As long as there have been human beings on this earth, there have been gods.

If you are human, you are a god-shaper. Rarely, a god or a goddess comes into view through the effort of a single individual acting alone. More commonly, the shaping of the divine requires many of us, joined in a shared culture, and working together over a great expanse of time.

If you are human, you are a god-shaper. But not a god-originator. We cannot create a god out of nothing, any more than a god can create us. We fashion them, form them, out of our divine imaginings, just as they fashion us, form us, in their turn. Mortal and immortal we shape one another.

If you are human, you are a god-shaper. Some choose to deny this role. Atheists and religious fundamentalists, in particular, deny their complicity in shaping the divine. Experience proves them both wrong. By eroding the claims of traditional theism, atheists have been among the most effective god-shapers of the last three centuries. By fighting a perpetual rear-guard action against that erosion, fundamentalists have remained vigorous god-shapers, narrowing their deities, fixing them in stone.

Between the atheists and the fundamentalists are the rest of us, occasionally apprehending the divine and then struggling to put a face on it.

Historically there have been two main modes for successful god-shaping: assertions of fact and suggestions of metaphor. The first mode asserts that a certain god is a provable entity in—or behind, or above—the universe, who has acted and still acts demonstrably in human history. The second mode suggests that a certain god is an ideal being, an embodiment of particular qualities or virtues, who acted long ago in mythic time and still acts metaphorically in the human soul.

Both sorts of god are thought to be "real." The factual god or goddess is real in the sense that the Pacific Ocean is real. It affects our weather, wears away the coastal rocks, supplies us with food...and fills us with awe. The metaphorical goddess or god is real in the sense that Beethoven's *Ninth Symphony* is real. It may thrill our senses, may alter our breathing, may shape our intellectual experience...and may fill us with awe.

Followers of a factual god typically put a great deal of stock in what one *believes*. There are creeds, dogmas, and catechisms spelling out what is or is not true with regard to the divine being. Two tribes, two nations may worship the same god but disagree as to specific beliefs about him. Often a holy war must be waged to settle the matter.

The factual god carries a particular burden, for he accumulates a vast array of literal assertions about his essential nature. These assertions come to command among believers the same unswerving allegiance originally given to the god himself. As such certainties multiply, they lead to difficult contradictions of fact, which trouble the very sort of person who finds the factual deity most congenial.

This multiplication of certainties is nowhere more apparent than in the development of "sacred scriptures"—texts that purport to be divinely inspired or indeed to have been written by the god himself. Within such texts, claims may be made about the deity, about humanity, or about nature that have no basis in human experience outside of the sacred scripture. These claims, however, because they "come from god," are taken by believers to be literal truth. The inevitable result is a radical split between what some believe to be true by faith and what others suspect to be true by reason, evidence, and experience.

Followers of a metaphorical god or goddess, by contrast, may know plenty of good stories about their deity but they do not learn them from a god-endorsed text. They possess no assertions of unassailable fact; no formal statements of dogma. The god or goddess may be seen, felt, sensed, intuited, visualized, loved, worshiped, thanked, petitioned, honored, or even excoriated by his or her human admirers. But without creed or catechism, that deity is never the object of their *belief*.

There was a time in the not-too-distant past when science and religion were on good terms. In an age of metaphorical gods, the physical world was sacred; the spiritual world made sense. With the ascendancy of a factual god came a parting of the ways. Science continued to see a dynamic reality waiting to be explored. Religion increasingly saw a fixed reality needing to be defended. Eventually these formerly close companions no longer spoke the same language. For centuries now, prominent followers of the factual god have taken human science as their enemy, picking fights that science has consistently won.

When people say, "God is dead," there can be little doubt as to which sort of god they mean. In our time the factual god suffers from his inability to act convincingly in the real world. Insofar as such a god still lives on, he lives on as metaphor.

B

BREAKING FREE

Some cultures have shown a greater talent for god-shaping than others. More often than not, individuals in such cultures enjoy a high degree of spiritual and intellectual freedom. Unfortunately our own culture is not as free as we think.

For well over a millennium, Western religious thought has been trapped in a box. The front and back of the box are the Torah and Mishna of Judaism. The left and right sides are the Koran and Sunna of Islam. The top and bottom are the Christian Gospels and the letters of Saint Paul.

Tiny air holes perforate the box on all six sides, allowing Hasidim and Sufis and Christian mystics a chance to breathe. But the box of monotheism seldom opens. Occasionally the top lifts just a crack—pried open perhaps by the Greco-Roman world in which Christianity was born. We glimpse a word or a phrase that hints at a larger spiritual universe: "In the beginning was the Logos." "The Kingdom of God is in your midst."

The Buddha, of course, lived outside the box, as did Confucius and Lao-Tzu and the writers of the Vedas, the Upanishads, and the Bhagavad-Gita. Neither Africa nor the Americas showed much interest in monotheism until they were vigorously "evangelized." But ancient Europe lived outside the box as well. Peoples as diverse as the Celts and the Teutons, the Etruscans and the Greeks all worshiped a host of deities. Polytheism has rightly been called the natural religion of humanity.

Today in the West, whether we call ourselves believers or doubters, evangelists or atheists, most of us understand "religion" to be what happens inside the box. We find it difficult or impossible to use the same term in the same sense when describing the beliefs and practices of polytheism, pantheism, or non-theism.

If our god-shaping is to be something more than a passive repetition of monotheism's "truths," we

8

may have to question many of our inside-the-box assumptions.

The first question will be the most fundamental: If the divine exists, is it singular or plural? Monotheism is confident of its answer. Are we ready to entertain other answers?

A second question may seem so easy that it need not be asked: Did God—or any god—create us? For monotheism this is self-evident. For other traditions, the answer varies from a flat denial (in ancient Greece) to a refusal to find the question meaningful (in ancient China).

Inside the box, we are certain that the laws or commandments of God are the principal sources of human morality. Belief in a divine being implies a certain code of moral conduct. Outside the box this is not so. Buddhism, for example, teaches a highly developed moral code without claiming divine authority for it. The ancient Greeks worshiped a highly developed pantheon without relying on the gods for their moral code.

Inside the box, we may understand such concepts as "original sin" and "atonement" and "salvation" and "eternal life" to be fundamental to a proper view of our lives in this world and beyond it. Outside the box, these terms will have entirely different meanings or no meaning at all. For many religions human life is not nearly as problematic as it is for monotheism. Humanity has not been broken. It is not in need of fixing.

Over the past century, while most people in the West seemed content to slumber inside the box, certain individuals managed to wake up and break free. Some turned to Asian religions and philosophies, others to the pre-monotheistic deities of Europe or Africa or the Americas, still others to modern psychology, which framed old religious concepts in useful new ways. Strikingly, even some monotheists began to embrace ideas and values that stretched traditional dogmas past their breaking point.

Such brave individuals, as they made their escape, left some sizeable holes in the box. We stand in their debt. Every soul that breaks free makes the way a little easier for the rest of us.

Γ

CLASSIC ADVICE

Let us for a moment try to imagine ourselves outside the box of monotheism. Let us assume that we are fully aware of our human creative power in a relationship that is not unidirectional but reciprocal. Let us try to shape an appealing, affirming, compelling, *and true* idea of the divine. What will we need?

1) We'll need a temperate climate. Allowing wide latitude for what may constitute "temperate," we must certainly exclude the dry tropical or sub-tropical desert. History shows that extreme climes breed extreme deities, with tendencies toward black-and-white, toward all-or-nothing, and worse still, toward us-versus-them. Desert gods are

likely to be "either/or" gods; temperate gods are likely to be "both/and."

2) We will need an intellectually free populace with open minds. Our gods will be only as open to possibility as we can imagine them. If we are, as a people, imaginatively circumscribed in some way, the best we may be capable of shaping is "an uncircumscribed deity." Having made the phrase, we will not have given the god a specific positive trait. Instead he is simply "not limited like us." It is similar to describing a god as "immortal" or "all-powerful" or "all-knowing." We start with our human limitations—death or impotence or ignorance—and then deny them in the divine. This is a beginning, but it is only a beginning.

3) We'll need poets, painters, musicians, playwrights, sculptors, dancers, architects, composers.... If our gods are to function successfully as ideal beings in a metaphorical world, we will need masters of metaphor to shape them. What we will clearly *not* need is a council of clerics. Our goal is not to define a deity and then freeze-dry him for all time. Rather we want our gods to be at least as capable of growth and evolution as are we.

4) We'll need to address the Mystery of Being, not ignore it. We are born into this mystery. Our very existence is a wonder, a marvel, and—because we

12

are human with an inborn need to ask "Why?" — it is a puzzle. As we mature, our parents, our siblings, our teachers, even our religious leaders conspire to dispel our wonder at the mystery, to solve the puzzle for us. This is not deliberate evil-doing but "education." Once we are educated the mystery is often obscured or worse, explained. But if this Mystery of Being were really explainable, it wouldn't continue generation after generation to be a mystery.

5) We will need to be open to divine moments. Remember the time when you sensed that a certain place was holy? Remember the song or songbird or hum of wind that seemed to transport you to a better reality? Remember returning the touch of your beloved with a love that felt more than temporal? Remember the radiant sunset that seemed too beautiful to be just a matter of earth rotation, light refraction, and retinal reception? Sometimes we say that in such moments we forget ourselves. There's a start. Now let us add that we remember the god.

6) And finally we'll need a pre-existing and widely shared idea of the divine on which to build. This is not a matter of humility; it is a matter of experience. Certainly our fertile brains are capable of conjuring up divinities out of little more than personal fantasy or wish fulfillment. But a

god idea gains both weight and resonance by living within a community of human souls over an extended period of time. Successful god-shaping requires a model, a precedent, or at the very least, a connection with some archetypal motif embedded within humanity. Acknowledging precursors on our path, far from placing a cap on the act of shaping, provides it with a foundation.

God-shaping is an art not a science. As in any great art form, a successful effort requires both inspiration and deliberation on the part of the artist. Our intuitions and even our intense experiences of the divine are not enough. We must apply at least a modicum of rational, purposeful thought to our work.

To speak of "a successful effort" is to imply that some ideas of the divine, like some works of art, may be judged qualitatively better than others. Such a claim stands or falls on the basis of tangible and intangible results in the human sphere, and on how we value those results.

To say, "This god is better shaped because He is the One True God," is obviously nonsense, since the only "evidence" for such a claim of fact lies in the belief system of those making the claim. To say, "This goddess is better shaped because her followers tend to be kind and gentle," is to make a claim that may be tested by experience: Are they kind and gentle? And then weighed against a common standard: Do we value kindness and gentleness; do we find these traits admirable or useful? As Jesus of Nazareth, one of the greatest god-shapers of all time has been quoted as saying, "By their fruits you shall know them."

Why do we suppose that our six suggestions will yield positive results? Because they have been tried at least once before—about three thousand years ago—with spectacular success. I believe we can find no better models for our own ventures into god-shaping than the deities shaped by ancient Greece.

This statement may startle some of you. You may know, or think you know enough about the Greek gods to dismiss them out of hand. Perhaps you regard them as entertaining subjects for art and literature but not as real deities worthy of serious worship. If that is your current opinion, please bear with me for just a bit longer.

Ask yourself, is it possible there may be more to the gods and goddesses of Greece than what you learned of them in school? Ask yourself, does it make sense that a people who showed such intelligence in other areas should have worshiped silly deities? Ask yourself, isn't it probable that what the Greeks *imagined* contributed in a meaningful way to what they *accomplished*?

Few historians would deny that ancient Greece produced the most intellectually fertile culture the West has known. I am asking you to consider a further claim: Ancient Greece produced the most spiritually insightful culture the West has known.

Let me emphasize that when I speak of Greek deities I mean the lively "gods of the poets" — Zeus and his family, the pantheon of Olympus. In the terms introduced above, these are "metaphorical" rather than "factual" beings. During the great age of Greece, every educated person could both enjoy the poetic retelling of the myths and worship these genuine gods. They saw no contradiction in this. They understood that what is well-imagined can also be real.

The Greeks could not have achieved what they achieved had they not imagined the gods they imagined. Yet beyond their value as a catalyst, the gods represent, in themselves, the Greeks' finest achievement. Once you step outside the box, these conclusions will cease to seem surprising and start to seem inevitable.

SHAPING GREEKS

Architecture, sculpture, painting, ceramics;

Instrumental music, vocal music, dance;

Diagnostics, medicine, pharmacology;

Geometry, mathematics, engineering;

Epic and lyric poetry, tragic and comic drama;

Government and law;

Athletic competition;

Logic, philosophy, metaphysics, science;

History, biography, fiction, criticism.

The Greeks excelled in each of these fields. More than that, they innovated in each. More than that, they often *invented* the field as we know it. Without question ancient Greece was one of the most creative civilizations in history.

Our list above skims the surface of an enormous sea. The Greek achievement is so wide and so deep that few of us today can fully comprehend it. But when we hear a choral ode of Sappho, or see a vase formed and painted by Exekias, or attend a performance of *Oedipus the King*, we glimpse one shining drop in the sea and may begin to intuit the immensity of the whole.

The more one learns, the more astonishing the Greeks appear. Here was a relatively small population whose independence from larger states lasted a relatively short time. Yet they became the tutors of Rome; and through Rome, of Europe; and through Europe, of half the world. We owe who we are today—in varying degrees—to Greece.

This is something everyone knows, or should know. But the expression "common knowledge" occasionally masks uncommon ignorance. Just as we have all learned something of the Greek achievement, we have all learned something of the Greek gods: they were fanciful, immoral, deceitful, changeable.... If the Greek people managed to do great things, they did so in spite of their rather primitive, rather frivolous religion.

Of course this is absurd. Yet it has been believed, vaguely or explicitly, by most people in the West for over a thousand years.

Our negative image of Greek religion derives in part from the ongoing arrogance of monotheism — a faith so unlike our own cannot be worth much. But the significance of the Greek gods had already been distorted in late antiquity by their Roman admirers as well as by their Christian detractors.

The Romans, in good polytheistic fashion, absorbed elements of Greek myth into their own myths and literature. But in almost every instance the transfer became a dilution. The immediacy and intensity of the Greek experience of the divine was transformed into a series of charming fairy tales. By contrast, the early Christians attacked "pagan" religion head on, offended both by the scandalous elements in the myths and by the apparent idolatry of worshiping sculpted gods and goddesses.

We have inherited both of these distortions. Yet if we take the trouble to look closely at what the Greeks actually did, we will find that their religion was not irrelevant to their accomplishments but indispensable to them. How could it be otherwise?

Consider Chartres Cathedral. Try to imagine the stained glass, the stone sculpture, or the building itself *without* the influence of Christianity. Consider Istanbul's Blue Mosque. Try to picture it *without* the influence of Islam. Now consider the Parthenon.

It was built as the principal temple in a sacred precinct. It was dedicated to Athena Parthenos (Virgin). And it housed a great statue of the goddess. No one should doubt that religion played a major part in its siting, its design, and its sculptural decoration.

The Parthenon is only the best-known example from scores of magnificent Greek temples, many of them still standing. Whether measured by size, beauty, financial cost, human effort, or civic significance, these were the most important

20

buildings of ancient Greece. They gave the architects of subsequent ages much to quote and more to ponder. They are what we mean when we say "Greek architecture." Without the gods they would not exist.

"Too easy," says the skeptic. "By their very nature, temples are likely to be monumental, public, and religious." Then let us move to the opposite pole in the visual arts—small, private, and secular—and look at painted pottery made for domestic use.

Anyone who has visited a major museum will have seen a painted Greek vase or cup. The number of excellent pieces still extant suggests the amazing number originally produced. Athens, Corinth, and other centers each had its own particular style of painting. Yet they all shared a common subject matter—the gods and heroes of myth. This was a cultural choice. The Greeks also imagined and painted harvest scenes and sporting events and children at play. But most often they imagined gods.

Nowhere did they imagine them more completely or more beautifully than in their freestanding statues of individual gods. Even today a bronze Apollo or a marble Aphrodite can confront us with such authority that we think, "I am meeting a deity here." Without these deities the Greek legacy in sculpture—as in architecture, as in painting—would simply be unimaginable.

When we turn from images to words, the pattern still holds: the gods are everywhere. Consider epic poetry and tragic drama, the two literary forms most closely identified with ancient Greece. In Homer's *Iliad*, set during the siege of Troy, the gods not only propel the action but also participate in it. Whole scenes are devoted to divine machinations on Olympus. In other scenes gods counsel human beings, make weapons for them, and even join in their battles. While the narrative focuses mainly on Achilles, Hector, and other men, the Olympians are much more than plot devices. Each deity is presented as a distinct character with personal motivations and personal reactions to events.

Tragic drama was a Greek invention. Though the form has inspired countless playwrights in later ages, nothing can match the power of those original tragedies. Aeschylus, Sophocles, and Euripides wrote their plays to be performed at a religious festival and in a space sacred to Dionysos. As in Homer, "the will of the gods"— or the will of a specific god—stands behind much of the human drama. Also as in Homer, the gods themselves may appear on stage, taking part in the action.   Frequently that action includes religious ritual, prayer, or divinely inspired dreams. Thus the context, the content, and often the characters in these plays are religious. How can one separate the stream from its source?

We could multiply examples that make the same case. Not only the visual arts but also music and dance were tied to religion, and gods filled the pages of Greek writers from Pindar to Pausanias. Yet "the Greek achievement" involved a great deal more than artistic creativity. Here, after all, were the foundations of Western philosophy, history, medicine, mathematics, and science.

These enterprises owed as much to Olympus as did the arts, but it was a different sort of debt. To the painter and poet the gods gave the gift of their own vivid personalities. To the philosopher and scientist they gave the gift of their reticence.

How does the human eye function? The gods say nothing. If A equals B, and B equals C, does A equal C? The gods are silent. Does the sun move round the earth or vice versa? No opinion.

By *not* providing a sacred scripture or a fixed dogma or a professional priesthood to define the proper limits of inquiry, the gods freed human beings to figure things out for themselves.

Herodotus could write a historical narrative without making it conform to a sacred text. Hippocrates could diagnose and treat a disease without searching for a supernatural cause or cure. Democritus could develop his atomic theory without consulting an ecclesiastical court.

It would be hard to overstate the value of the gods' reticence. Yet they did much more than simply stand aside. While silent about the particular issues under investigation, they spoke loudly and clearly about the human capacity to investigate.

Greeks were not haunted by the "Fall of Man." No myth warned them away from the "Tree of Knowledge." On the contrary, their myths often told of gods granting specific gifts of knowledge to humans. Some of these were entirely practical —how to spin, how to weave, how to tame horses, how to cultivate olives. Others were more abstract —understanding music or mathematics. Still others—such as prophecy or the power to heal— blurred the usually sharp distinction between mortal and immortal knowing.

The gods also led by their example. Before teaching a particular skill or technique to humankind, the deity may have been responsible for discovering or inventing it. Often the god embodied in his or her person a special capability that the knowledge-seeker could emulate, as Athena embodied learning; or Hermes embodied invention; or Apollo, healing.

Equally important, the gods collectively sanctified the whole of the natural world. Their origins in nature, their associations with nature—and in the person of Artemis, their embodiment of nature—signified to any alert Greek that the natural world was eminently worthy of admiration and investigation.

Here we see something unique in the history of religion: an idea of the divine that not only tolerates human questions about our physical selves and our physical environment but also actively encourages these questions. How could a people with such gods *fail* to innovate? How could they *not* astonish the world?

And why stop with the arts and sciences? The Greeks invented a number of political and social institutions as well. Some of their creations—such as the mini-state called a *polis* and the elaborate annual festivals of that *polis*—did not outlast the Greek civilization. Others—such as the protection of free speech and trial by a jury of one's peers—remain key components of modern law.

Two Greek inventions continue to transform human lives: democracy and the Olympic Games.

While neither our current democracies nor our current games exactly conform to their Greek models, their lineage is clear and the benefits we derive from them echo those enjoyed in ancient Athens and Olympia.

They are not such an odd pair as you might think. In each case a large number of citizens (all Athenians / all Greeks) assembled in a dedicated place (the Pnyx hill / Olympia) to engage as equals in a controlled competition (for votes / for the olive crown) under the protection of a deity (Athena / Zeus).

Both democracy and the games presupposed an extraordinary level of competence in their participants. The one required an educated and agile mind, the other a trained and agile body. If citizens were less than exemplary in their citizenship, democracy failed. If runners were less than fully prepared, the race was lost. In both situations the group's success depended upon the effort and excellence of every individual. What a high opinion of themselves the Greeks must have had, to create this sort of government, this sort of competition!

They did have a high opinion of themselves and of humans in general. We know its source. The Greeks had shaped their gods to look like ideal human beings. Then they gazed upon those gods as in a mirror, and saw themselves perfected. Goethe said that the goal of the Greeks was not to humanize deity but to deify humanity. Few other mortals have come so close.

E

DIVINE COMPANY: AT HOME

You return home from school. You return home from work. You return home from a vacation.

If you are fortunate, the experience of returning comforts you. Home feels familiar, cozy, safe. Home and hearth are seldom thought to be exciting. That they are unexciting is a great part of their charm. Yet the ancient Greeks, god-shapers *par excellence*, recognized in home and hearth something more than familiarity, something more than safety. For them the home was a divine precinct and returning home was a holy act of pilgrimage. Of their twelve principal deities, one —Hestia—is devoted solely to hearth and home.

Now for many of us alive today a hearth is a luxury, a decorative adjunct to our gas or electric furnace. Perhaps the modern kitchen, not the fireplace, is as close as we can come to the ancient idea of a hearth. But many of us treat the kitchen as just an unavoidable pit stop on the road race of our lives. And our home itself may be a "machine for living in," nothing more. If we conceive of our real life as lived elsewhere, then this ancient idea that the home is so holy that it demands its own presiding goddess will have no resonance.

The work we accomplish out in the world we usually consider to be genuine work. The work we accomplish at home we consider merely chores. The mother who takes an outside job we call "a working mother," as though the one who rears children at home were not. Financial compensation helps draw this spurious line in our minds, compelling us to confuse intrinsic value with market value.

But our mundane home-based chores, as well as the homebound duties of child rearing, are fully necessary to our human lives, as necessary in their way as earning a living. It was the genius of the ancient Greeks to see in these necessary human activities an element of holiness, to celebrate them, and to worship the goddess who was (and remains) their patron.

Ask yourself what constitutes your "real life?" Is it so different in its essential elements from that of the ancients? Most of us leave home each day to work, to earn, to learn, to socialize, to engage in the activities of our community, however we define community. Our public lives, our lives outside the home are not more meaningful to us, surely, than their lives in the *agora* and *palaestra* were to the ancient Greeks.

The ancients show us that no contradiction need exist between placing a high value on our public lives and an equally high value on our private lives. We may celebrate our away-from-home experiences for their richness, variation, tension, and for our sense of making a mark in the world. But equally, we should celebrate our within-the-home experiences for their relative simplicity, repetition, quiet, and for our sense of renewal.

Imagine for a moment that your home is a holy place. Imagine that a friendly goddess presides over that place and your deeds in it. Imagine that those deeds — the eating, the sleeping, the cooking, the cleaning — are a series of sacred acts that are performed with respect for the place and for its goddess.

Your home is still the same but it is now more. You have transformed it from just another place into *the place*. You have simultaneously improved your own life and helped to shape the ancient goddess Hestia.

Z

DIVINE COMPANY: AT WORK

Homo Faber — Man the Maker, the Fabricator. First, human beings made tools. Then we used our tools to fashion "shoes and ships and sealing wax," pyramids of stone, chips of silicon, and all the other *stuff* of our lives. In the present age we make tools of such sophistication that they enable us to make other, still-more-sophisticated tools. We have learned from the Greeks to call this activity "technology." We have not yet learned from the Greeks to call this activity sacred.

The hard-muscled god Hephaistos works with hammer and anvil at his forge, beating hot metal into a thousand useful and beautiful shapes. He is the patron of all craftsmen, manufacturers, technologists, and by extension of all workers. When a child folds paper to make an airplane; when a rocket engineer adjusts a trajectory to put a satellite into orbit; each is—or could be— honoring the god by such an act.

In our culture and in our time we are seldom inclined to associate our work, and specifically our acts of making, with the divine. Indeed it is common now in the West to draw a line between sacred times and activities (e.g. Sunday worship at a church) and profane times and activities (e.g. Monday through Friday labor at an auto plant).

The Greeks knew no such separation. Certainly they had sacred places—holy sites, temples, shrines. And certainly they had sacred times—the festival of a god, the solstice, the dawn of a new day. But their boundaries between sacred and profane times, places, or activities were tissue thin compared to ours, and the interpenetration of the immortal and the mortal realms was an acknowledged fact of life. Daily life.

The smith at his forge, the mason at his wall, the net-maker, the potter, the weaver all labored under the patronage of Hephaistos. In their daily activities, their making, they could work for his

34

approval, ask for his aid, offer the products of their labor and the labor itself as a gift to their patron. This may not have made their work any better; it made it more meaningful.

Our culture suffers from a very considerable error, one that we share unfortunately with many cultures of the past: we look for the divine in the super-natural, the extra-ordinary. The Greek religious genius discovered, conversely, a very great truth: the divine is present in the most natural things, in the most ordinary activities.

Human making, human working—it's what we humans do. It would have been wholly alien to the Greek conception of the divine to separate something so essential to our humanity from its sacred dimension.

But are we not capable of a similar fusion in our own time? If we choose we may imagine Hephaistos designing and making integrated circuits or optical fiber. It matters little how we bend the metaphor, so long as the essential intuition remains—our work is a series of sacred acts watched over by a work-wise god.

H

DIVINE COMPANY: ON THE LAND

All of us must eat to live. Some of us live to eat. But few of us grow our own dinner. We haven't lost our intimacy with food but with its source.

Oh, we know where our food comes from: the refrigerator. Before that, the supermarket. Before that, a big truck. Before that...?

Most of us live a long way from those fertile, cultivated fields where our grains are planted and harvested; those lush orchards where our fruits ripen in the sun; those green pastures where our cattle slowly mature into fast food. Our farmers have become agri-businessmen, employing a huge work force on vast estates. And we have become their markets, a mass of "consumers."

Just as we are removed in space from the land where our food is grown, we are removed in time from the cycle of planting and harvesting. Was the cereal on my breakfast table made from winter wheat or summer wheat? Was this orange picked in March in Florida or in May in the Canary Islands?

The World Farm feeds the World City. And if our particular sector of the city has enough ready cash, there's no need to worry about a bad harvest. We read of floods in California; strawberries and artichokes will cost a bit more this year. There's a drought in Colombia; how much will we pay for a good cup of coffee?

But a few of us still are real farmers and a few more still tend gardens of their own. These are the fortunate ones, because as they plant and cultivate, tend and harvest, they experience first-hand the connections between seed and soil and sun and water. And they may well observe a further link—between their humanity and the earth that sustains it.

Like most peoples before our time, the Greeks knew these connections well. Like most peoples before our time, they feared famine and worked vigorously to avoid it. The goddess whom they praised in times of bounty and petitioned in times of want they called Demeter, goddess of the grain, of the fertile field, of the harvest. Because she was goddess of the fruitful earth, Demeter also watched over the progress of the seasons.

We may see her hand still in an early spring or in a long autumn. But few of us now collaborate with Demeter "in the field." Even fewer can celebrate her at the moment of harvest. We know the land is fertile *somewhere*, we know *some* harvest was good, because of what comes finally to our table. When we sit down to a meal, though we cannot trace a single item on our plate back to its source in the earth, we know that its source is, ultimately, of the earth.

Mealtime thus is the one moment in the present age when most of us may encounter Demeter, the generous goddess—not by working with her but by enjoying her bounty. At this moment methods of agriculture and systems of distribution are irrelevant. Our sustenance is a gift of the goddess. And every meal we enjoy is potentially a sacred meal, a thanksgiving.

DIVINE COMPANY: ON THE SEA

Have you been to the ocean? Have you been *on* the ocean? Anyone who has experienced that vast, uncontrollable immensity should have no difficulty seeing the divine in it.

The Greeks called the god of the sea Poseidon and found in him all that you would expect of such a god. He was patron of sailors and fishermen, the one who sent squalls or brought calm water. They petitioned Poseidon before every voyage and gave him thanks upon reaching safe harbor.

Glance at a map of Greece and you will see why Poseidon was, for the inhabitants of that landscape of peninsulas and islands, a very great god indeed. The sea was their context—always for trade, often for war, sometimes for exploration and expansion.

41

The sea is our context as well, but a more abstract one. Unlike the majority of ancient Greeks, many of us go through entire years without glimpsing the sea. But even the inhabitants of Moscow and Minneapolis realize that what happens on distant seas can affect their weather for a day or for a decade. Each of us knows that the ocean covers more than seventy percent of our planet, and most of us accept the idea that the origins of all life on the planet were found in that great world-ocean.

Just as farmers and gardeners may know Demeter more intimately than the rest of us, seafarers and sailors will come closer on a daily basis to Poseidon. Yet "intimacy" is not the right word to describe our human interaction with this sometimes benign, sometimes terrible god. For he is not so much a god of water—the compound of hydrogen and oxygen—as he is of so great a body of water. For Poseidon, size matters.

Poseidon lives in the sheer vastness, the breathtaking immensity of the ocean (not in its *wetness*). The Greeks made this clear by his other attributes. They saw not a trace of him in ponds or springs or streams; but he spoke in the rumble of earthquakes and the thundering hooves of horses.

Though Demeter also works "large," regulating the cycle of seasons, we meet her most often in the intimacy of a thumb pressing a seedling into soil or a tongue tasting a morsel of fruit. By contrast, we almost always encounter Poseidon with a sense of awe.

Awe—a mixture of reverence, exhilaration, and terror—is a rare emotion for us. All sorts of noises envelop our lives and penetrate our souls, drowning out the pounding surf, let alone the lapping waves of the god. Such distractions are not new for humankind but they steadily become worse.

Poets and painters of an earlier age actively sought to reinvigorate the emotion of awe by embracing what they called "the sublime." We are no longer Romantics, but we share their need for wonder and dread. And despite the noise, we may still sometimes imagine ourselves in a very small boat rocking in the midst of a shoreless sea.

I

DIVINE COMPANY: IN LOVE

She is beautiful. She is desirable. She is seductive. She is the deity who needs no introduction: Aphrodite, goddess of love and physical beauty. Two thousand years of monotheism in the West have not diminished her power nor erased her name. How could they? We are human; we love.

We love our lovers in a multitude of ways — passionately, decorously, brutally, tenderly, wisely, foolishly — and Aphrodite sanctions them all. But the ancient Greeks, who knew her first, thought of her primarily in terms of irresistible, uncontrollable desire. She was for them, and remains for us the motivator of two persons inexorably drawn to one another, body to body, skin to skin, mouth to mouth....

Her followers may be heterosexual, homosexual, bisexual, or pansexual but they are never asexual. For Aphrodite has nothing to do with what has been termed "spiritual love" or "fraternal love." Her love is sexual through and through. Consequently, her chief holy rite is not marriage but the physical act of lovemaking itself.

Apparently this offended the Fathers of the Christian Church. Those whose view of human sexuality remains tied to the dogmas of monotheism may still find Aphrodite's message hard to swallow. Sex is—in itself, by itself—holy. For the rest of us, what a wonderful concept! Young or old, inside or outside marriage, in the bedroom, on the kitchen table, in the woods, underwater, you name it: making love is itself divine, a holy act of worship.

Anyone who has shared the sheer exhilaration of "falling in love," the wonder and sickness of "being in love," the intense physical joy and release of "making love," will grasp the terrible power of this great goddess. When she takes hold of us, our world is transformed. Our views of others, our behavior, our goals are not what they were. We live—some for a moment, some for a lifetime—"under the aspect of love."

If, transfixed by her power, we give ourselves exclusively to this sexy goddess, ignoring every other deity, we are certain to shatter our lives. For to say that human desire is always holy is not to say that it is always wise. Second thoughts, sober reflections are none of Aphrodite's concern. She simply turns us on, leaving it to others to pick up the pieces. Fortunately we have all those other gods to turn to when we need them.

K

DIVINE COMPANY: AT WAR

Is making war, like making love, a normal and necessary part of human existence? What do you say? However much we would like to think of war as an aberration, history suggests that it is the norm—not a constant state of war, thank the gods, but a continual recurrence of that state.

Visionaries throughout human history have dreamed of a permanent age of peace. Yet the reality for humankind has been that periods of peace have resulted from temporary moments of equilibrium between tribes or among nations. Two states are equally weak perhaps, or equally powerful; or one state is so very powerful that no other may challenge it, and so prosperous or indolent that it seeks no expansion. Such moments of equilibrium have always proved unstable.

During the last century more voices than ever claimed, "It need not be so." And during the last century more human beings died in wars than in all the centuries before.

For the ancient Greeks the certainty of war was a fact of life. They fought tremendous defensive wars against the encroaching power of Persia, as well as numerous aggressive wars among themselves. It was as natural for them to have a god of war, Ares, as to have a goddess of love. To be sure, these two deities did not elicit the same level of devotion. But you need not be fond of a god in order to honor him, to call on him, or to recognize his power.

Preparing for war, going to war, and in the heat of battle, we want Ares on our side. He is the warrior personified, whether we imagine him carrying a short sword and round shield or manning the guns of a fighter jet. He is master of the technical skills of combat, of strategy, of weaponry. Just as crucially, he is master of the appropriate attitude for engaging the enemy.

To a contemporary god-shaper, Ares may reveal more about ancient religion than any other god. If war is a necessary part of human existence, then Ares is a necessary deity. While he may not inspire our love, he does command our respect. Moreover, his high place within the Greek pantheon tells us that armed combat, though bloody and painful, partakes of the divine.

This is not "holy war" in the sense of a Christian crusade or an Islamic *jihad*, sanctified by the righteousness of the warriors' cause. This is war itself understood as holy in itself — the human energy, strength, and skills brought to bear; but also the loss of life, the suffering, the inevitable destruction — regrettable, hideous, yet holy.

Λ

DIVINE COMPANY: IN THE CITY

Athena is our divine teacher. In the distant past, according to the Greeks, she taught humanity the skills we needed in order to become civilized. She taught women to cook, to weave, and to spin; she taught men how to tame horses, how to plough, how to build. She invented musical instruments ...and mathematics.

Implicit in all of these specifics, of course, was her greatest gift—the stimulation of human reason. The Greeks looked to her, more than to any other deity, for good counsel in matters both practical and theoretical. She came to embody the very idea of wisdom.

She was patron and protector of Athens, the city named for her and a major force in the flowering of ancient Greek civilization. Indeed, two thousand five hundred years after its golden age, ancient Athens continues to define the word "civilization" for the West.

There is more than a casual connection between the nature of the city's goddess and the extent of the city's achievement. The Athenians were, like their divine patron, both inventive and thoughtful. Their prodigious intellectual and literary and artistic products—created within a tiny state and in a relatively brief time—continue to educate and inspire the world. History tells us that the Athenians were not always wise in foreign policy, nor always just in internal politics. But they managed as a society to be experimental, testing their own laws, practices, and policies against actual experience and in the light of reason.

What an extraordinary phenomenon in the ancient world! What a refreshing phenomenon it would be today! Reason remains, at best, one voice among many in the arrangement of our public affairs, and seldom is it the dominant one.

This is not to say that Athena has entirely disappeared from our lives. She is honored today —sometimes even by name—in centers of learning

54

and research. Modern society appears to have enormous respect for rational inquiry as long as it knows its place. Clearly that place is no longer at the very core of our public life.

And what about our *private* lives? Are you a reasonable, thoughtful person? Do you aspire to be? To what extent do your actions and words issue from a balanced weighing of alternatives? Can you imagine yourself calling upon the goddess to help you be just a tad more reflective? Just a trifle wiser?

Like the other deities of Greece, Athena embodies something inside us as well as something out there. She reminds us that this peculiarly human faculty of reason holds an ember of divine fire. She challenges us to fan that ember.

During the last century a great deal was written about the "limits of reason" and about our need to supplant purely rational, "linear" thinking with elements of intuition, spontaneity, or mysticism. This was odd on two counts. First, because no society and very few individuals had ever seriously tested the upper limits of the human power of rational thought. Second, because no one had ever seriously believed that reason alone could answer all our personal or societal problems.

Athena is a very great goddess and her gifts to us have been enormous. Yet no Greek, not even an Athenian, would have claimed that she was the *only* goddess.

M

DIVINE COMPANY: ON THE ROAD

A god-shaper's riddle: What do a pile of stones, a pair of winged sandals, a ram, a lyre, and a herald's staff have in common? Not much, one would think, except that all are signs of the god Hermes, a complex figure indeed.

Like his fellow deities, he evolved—that is, he was shaped—over time. His earliest manifestations may have been the heaps of stones placed at crossroads or used to mark paths. (*Herma* is the Greek word for a pile of stones.) Poets expanded on this association with roads. In some of their tales Hermes acted as a helpful guide; in others he was a cunning trickster. Naturally enough, he became the protector of all travelers—but also the protector of thieves.

He appeared in the Greek myths more often than any other deity, usually conveying messages from one god to another or from a god to a mortal. As the "divine herald" he carried a herald's staff and wore winged sandals to speed him on his many journeys. Of course he became the patron of oratory and rhetoric.

Hermes was always in motion and not even the clever Greeks could pin him down to a single role. He was their god of commerce, friend of traders and merchants. Simultaneously he was patron of athletes. He sent dreams to living mortals and escorted the dying to the realm of the dead. He invented the lyre and the shepherd's pipe. As the chief protector of shepherds and the guardian of their flocks, Hermes was often pictured as "the good shepherd" himself, carrying a ram on his shoulders.

God-shaping can be fun. But while we marvel at the wonderful richness of this god's mythology, we can also see some common threads. Hermes is a god of communications in the broadest sense. Most of his attributes cluster around forms of movement or forms of speech, and his central role as herald combines the two. At the same time he is the consummate mediator, moving easily between gods and men, between waking and sleep, between life and death.

The Greeks wisely trusted reason more than rhetoric. Accordingly, if they saw Athena as a solid citizen, they saw Hermes as a bit of a rogue. He was famous for his powers of persuasion, but also famous for not always telling the whole truth.

Some folks today will find it surprising that a god—who is, after all, an ideal being, worthy of our honor and worship—may be capable of trickery, of theft, and of fudging the facts. Hermes doubtless is capable of all three. This aspect of the god underscores the intimate link between the Greeks' conception of divinity and their conception of humanity.

The gods they shaped, like the humans who worshiped them, sometimes behaved morally but sometimes did not. The gods could indeed set standards of morality, but occasionally they themselves failed to meet them.

Perhaps equally telling, the gods could mess about. "Sacred" for the Greeks did not equal "somber." If the gods could be playful—what a divine idea!—human beings could play as well, and feel good about it.

Nowadays when we want to get from here to there, or when we want to find the right word, Hermes is our god. He is the divine in transit, equally at home ambling along a country road or speeding along the "information superhighway." We may call upon him as we book our vacations or when we write our blogs. He is busy in the world of commerce, dealing fairly (most of the time). He is active in our courts of law, arguing honestly (most of the time). He is patron of our journalists, who sometimes bend the truth, and of our politicians, who nearly always do.

At a deeper level, we may look to Hermes in his role as mediator to help us with our own crossings. He is the god most likely to speak to us about divine matters. He is the god who shapes our dreams, connecting our conscious and unconscious selves. And he promises to be our eventual guide over the threshold of death.

N

DIVINE COMPANY: IN NATURE

The child emerging from its mother's womb is born into two worlds at once. One we call "nature;" the other, "culture."

These two spheres complement one another and interpenetrate one another throughout our lives. Culture — first in the form of our parents, teachers, and peers; later through our experience of the arts, sciences, rites, and laws of our society — informs our conceptions of nature. Similarly, nature — first in the form of our genetic make-up, but later through our encounters with specific landscapes, climates, plants and animals — informs our conceptions of culture.

We come to know that culture exists entirely *within nature*, in the sense that all humans are animals and that all of the behaviors of our species are thus natural phenomena. But we also learn that nature, as it is apprehended by human minds and constructed by human societies, may be said to exist entirely *within culture*.

The Greeks recognized the divine in wild nature and called her Artemis. They recognized the divine in human culture and called him Apollo. In a stroke of god-shaping genius, their myths describe Artemis and Apollo not only as sister and brother but also as *twins*. Both are archers and both are pictured as young, athletic, and beautiful.

The virgin Artemis lives in forests, on mountainsides, in all of the wild places beyond human cultivation. The Greeks imagined her as a lithe hunter and patron of hunters, but also as the protector of the young of all species. She was said to help women in childbirth, but also to bring sudden death with her unerring arrows.

These core traits of Artemis reveal an essential truth about every Greek deity: the god or goddess is simultaneously a vividly imagined divine being and a complex metaphor.

Artemis is a virgin because she represents nature pure and whole, uncompromised by the assaults of man. She is petitioned especially during childbirth and at the approach of death—that is, at the extremes of human life, when we come out of and return to raw "uncultured" nature. In her relations with human beings she is sometimes kind, sometimes terrible. But she never ceases to be beautiful.

One of her most popular myths concerns the hunter Actaeon, who accidentally came upon her and her attendant nymphs while they bathed naked in a forest stream. Artemis abruptly turned poor Actaeon into a stag; his own hunting dogs soon tore him to bits.

Now if you take this story literally, it seems appallingly unjust—a blameless hunter punished for his innocent mistake by a vengeful goddess. But read as metaphor the myth contains an important truth. Nature will punish the incursions of man upon her sanctity, regardless of whether they are unwitting or deliberate.

Each of us individually, and all of us collectively may find ourselves transgressing upon the natural world. When we destroy a forest, pollute a river, or "develop" a field—even if we perceive our motive to be economic necessity—we should not be surprised when nature takes her revenge.

Yet Artemis, like every Greek deity, is more than the sum of her metaphors. She is a dynamic goddess, specifically imagined—young, active, skilled, free. Her attributes are equally specific: her bow and arrow, her accompanying doe, her identification with the full or crescent moon. Even her attire is clearly defined. The short tunic, the sandals, the quiver at her shoulder—each is necessary to her very particular life in nature.

The Greeks' talent for god-shaping could have no more apt or attractive exemplar. They have given us a goddess of all nature but imagined her as an active young woman moving about freely and purposefully within her wild domain.

She is both general and specific in just the ways our human interactions with nature are both general and specific. We may contemplate "nature naturing," the totality of our physical environment, and see ourselves as wholly immersed in her holy realm. Or we may hear a robin's song, see a falling leaf, or feel a fresh breeze, and find Artemis in the singularity of each particular encounter with the natural world.

When we confront nature's terrors, Artemis sees and sometimes allays our fears. When we are exhilarated by nature's beauty, she accepts our gratitude. And when we find ourselves awed by nature's mystery, she occasionally inspires in us a creative response to that mystery.

DIVINE COMPANY: IN CULTURE

When Artemis inspires us, Apollo, her twin brother, helps us shape that inspiration into significant form. He is the divine patron of the arts, god of music, dance, poetry, prose, painting, sculpture, architecture.... The Greeks called him "leader of the muses" and imagined him singing his own poems while accompanying himself on the lyre.

Like his sister, Apollo is a skilled archer, far-seeing, straight-shooting, and invariably on target. But compared to his virgin twin he is a walking scandal. The plentiful accounts of his erotic adventures suggest that the Greeks anticipated by some three thousand years our conjoining of libido and creativity.

Ancient artists and poets pictured Apollo as a handsome young man, strong, athletic, ideally proportioned—but also wise. Among the whole company of radiant Olympian deities, he is the one they particularly associated with light and identified with the sun.

He is credited with teaching the Greeks the two precepts most famously characteristic of their culture: "Know yourself" (that is to say, "Know that you mortal; understand what this entails.") and "Nothing in excess" (that is to say, "Practice moderation in everything you do.")

Both of these injunctions were inscribed upon his temple at Delphi, home of the most revered oracle of the ancient world. Myth and cult made Apollo the primary god of prophecy as well as the god most closely associated with rites of purification.

Finally, and very significantly, he was the chief god of healing, patron of medicine and physicians. It is this last function that helps us see the element common to all: Apollo is a god of health.

Himself the embodiment of physical perfection, he sponsors the healing arts to promote the physical health of all humanity. Through music, literature, art, and architecture he fosters our psychic health.

And by giving us the benefit of his precepts, rites, and prophecy, he protects our societal health.

While the Greeks associated Artemis with the whole of nature, they saw her most clearly in nature's wild beauty. Similarly, though prepared to find value in every aspect of human culture, they identified humanity's most beautiful creations with Apollo. He represents what is measured, balanced, well-proportioned, and whole, both in society and in the individual. He moves us to respond to what is best in our cultural environment and in ourselves. He inspires us to our own excellence.

Just as our assaults upon the natural world are offenses against Artemis, our cultural failures are offenses against her brother. We may easily recognize and condemn the failures that arise out of mass hysteria such as iconoclasm or book burning. More insidious are our daily "sins of omission" such as a preference for bread and circuses when we are capable of so much more.

Individually and collectively we often find it congenial just to get by. Apollo's divine presence stands as a constant admonition to each of us: "You must change your life."

What a triumph of the god-shaper's art! Apollo makes explicit what we find implicit in all the other deities of ancient Greece: the divine beings above us are metaphors for the divine within us. Apollo is our best ideas; he is our most worthy creations; he is the embodiment of our striving to fulfill, in this life, what it can mean to be human.

O

DIVINE COMPANY: IN EACH OTHER

"The divine lives within you."   For many of us
this simple statement expresses a profound truth.
We assent to it readily with a feeling of
exhilaration. No wonder then that this idea
appears again and again in the history of the
world's religions. Far rarer, because far more
challenging, is its corollary: "The divine lives also
within others."

When a Hindu greets a stranger with a reverential
bow, his palms pressed together in an attitude of
prayer, he is said to be acknowledging the sacred
"Self" within the stranger. Though the ancient

71

Greeks did not use that gesture or that term, they embraced a related concept. For them the connections between one human being and another were divine — or could become so. Beginning with a powerful belief in the essential worth of each individual person, they recognized that something transcendent occurs when two persons join together in friendship, in erotic love, or especially in marriage.

The divine embodiment of the holy state of matrimony was the marriage of Zeus and Hera —"first couple" among the gods. Zeus ruled Olympus; therefore his lawful spouse Hera was called the "Queen of Heaven." All of Greece worshiped her, both as the consort of the supreme god and in her own right, as patron of mortal women. Naturally enough, Hera became the protector of marriage.

Myths portray the divine marriage as a stormy one. Tale after tale tells of Zeus's infidelities and Hera's jealous responses. If one were to treat these tales as theology, one would have to say that this marriage made in heaven could never stand as a model for human imitation.

Yet nothing better illustrates the clear distinction between myth and cult in ancient Greece. The many cities that made Hera their patron goddess, the great temples built at Olympia, Argos, and Samos in her honor, the annual public rites in celebration of the "sacred marriage"—all attest to a genuine devotion to this goddess and to a genuine respect for the heavenly pair *as* a pair.

This disparity between myth and cult was hardly unique to the ancients. We may find a parallel in the medieval mystery plays, which often departed from dogma. For instance, the Biblical tale of a great flood sent by an angry god might devolve into repartee between drunken Noah and his shrewish wife. But because the Church vigorously defined and defended its canonical teachings during the Middle Ages, a playwright's fantasies offered little threat to the cult.

The Greeks, lacking a dogma or a holy book, lived on shakier theological ground. This was Plato's principal complaint against "the poets:" by telling a good story, they might distort or disfigure rather than enhance our notions about the gods. Let every god-shaper beware!

However entertaining—or sadly true-to-life—the Greeks may have found their tales about Zeus and Hera, they surely did not lose respect either for the institution of marriage or for the deities who embodied it. We know from Greek literature that they recognized marriage and the family as the bedrock of social organization, underpinning (and pre-dating) their political achievements. We know from Greek art that they also valued the intimacy, respect, and love involved in marital relations.

Today we are no less dependent on the communal utility of marriage as an *institution*. But with the geographical dispersion of families and our modern patterns of social interaction, we may be even more dependent than the Greeks were on marriage as a *relationship*.

One early poet (to whom not even Plato could object) called Hera "chief among the immortals in beauty." Those of us fortunate enough to be happily married will find ourselves in full agreement. Hera was not, is not a "babe" like the seductive Aphrodite. She was not, is not a taut-muscled teen like the sporty Artemis. Hers is the beauty of shared experience, the beauty of deep friendship, the beauty of mutual forgiveness, the beauty of abiding love.

Hera may grant us moments of volcanic passion but such eruptions are not her usual style. More typically, she generates a steady flame—with luck, an eternal one—which provides both warmth and light to those whom she blesses. But while we give her thanks for the continual joy of connecting deeply with another human being (and while we pray for her aid during the rough patches), we must remember that it is not Hera's blessing that sanctifies human marriage.

On the contrary, the goddess blesses our marriages because they are in themselves sacred.

Π

DIVINE COMPANY: IN THE COSMOS

A cerulean sky, cottony clouds along the horizon, a light breeze from the south: "Zeus is smiling."

Howling winds, driving rain, a rumble of thunder and crack of lightning: "Zeus is angry."

More than three thousand years ago, the early Greeks began to shape their supreme deity. Originally Zeus was their sky god, the bringer of rain, the impregnator of the fertile earth. Early on they identified his power with the thunderbolt. His totem was the eagle. His sacred tree, the spreading oak.

Not a bad beginning. From the realm of Zeus came the weather that informed daily life—when to plant, when to harvest, when to begin a journey, when to wage war. Concurrently the dome of the sky at night defined the outer limits of the visible world, providing a ready metaphor for the universe as a whole.

During the next millennium Zeus gradually evolved into a god of governance. He became the guarantor of human justice, the dispenser of divine mercy. He also became, in himself, a symbol for the ordered cosmos. Although we cannot recapture the thoughts and experiences of the innumerable Greeks who took part in this evolution, we can identify a few of their culture's more purposeful acts of god-shaping.

The early mythmakers were faulted by later philosophers for describing their sky god's dalliances with a host of local nymphs. In fact, such myths helped to frame the idea of a divine extended family with Zeus at its head. Homer presents a Zeus who protects supplicants and strangers, while punishing those who lie or break their oaths. Hesiod speaks of Zeus bringing justice to mankind. In the plays of Aeschylus, Zeus defines the moral laws of the universe. By the end of the Greek era, he is hailed as "Our

Zeus, the giver of every good gift, the common father and savior and guardian of mankind."

Complementing these god-shaping creations of the poets were those of painters, sculptors, and architects. Each time an image of Zeus appeared —whether as a great temple statue or as a small figure painted on a vase—the new image helped to refine its viewer's conception of the god.

Many early depictions show a Zeus of commanding power and vigor, hurling his terrible thunderbolt against a foe. Later he often appears as a judge or ruler, majestic and frontal, in the center of the scene. At the height of the classical age, Pheidias sculpted for the temple at Olympia a large statue of Zeus enthroned that was said to enlighten and transform those who stood before it.

This god whom so many ancient artists shaped, and ultimately passed on to us, is an impressive being indeed. More powerful than all the other gods put together, he is the particular protector of the weak among mankind. He is a constant threat to those who do evil but a rewarder of those who do good. He is a wise judge, frequently preferring mediation to the exercise of his awesome power. He is the prime exemplar of sound government, ruling justly over both gods and men.

One of the most extraordinary things about Zeus's rule, however, is that it is not absolute. The poets show him sometimes outsmarted by another god, sometimes defied by a mere mortal, and sometimes subject to an implacable "Fate" whose power he cannot circumvent or overcome. Thus his divine decrees *usually* carry the day; his will is *almost* law.

Now here is a liberating idea: a Supreme Being who is not always supreme. Olympus, the home of the gods, was no democracy. But an argument can be made that Zeus's strong, yet limited governance in heaven provided a rough model when certain enterprising Greeks began to develop their own firmly ordered, yet limited form of government on earth.

Perhaps equally surprising for those accustomed to monotheism, Zeus can *change*—change his mind, change his methods, and frequently change his physical form. The myths are full of his striking metamorphoses. Here he becomes an eagle; there a white bull. Now he pours himself down in a shower of gold; then he appears as a dark, enveloping cloud. No other god undergoes so many transformations.

Similarly his will, even when it is clear and sovereign, remains flexible. Another god may convince him to alter it; an offending mortal may sometimes find pardon. Longstanding laws may be subject to revision, should the reasons for such revision prove sufficiently powerful.

What a brilliant god! The same Zeus who represents the harmonious structure of the world is also a god of perpetual change. The universe he governs is both ordered and continually evolving. Zeus is eternal but not static; immortal but not fixed in form. He is as permanent as the starry sky and as unpredictable as the weather.

P

THE TWELVE

Hestia and Hephaistos

　　　　　Demeter and Poseidon

Aphrodite and Ares

　　　　　Athena and Hermes

Artemis and Apollo

　　　　　Hera and Zeus

As shaped by the ancient Greeks, each of these six goddesses and six gods is a distinct being, capable of independent action. Yet all are members of one divine family and occasionally act in concert.

Two generations live together on Olympus. The five elders include Zeus, his wife Hera, his sisters Demeter and Hestia, and his brother Poseidon.

The younger seven are all children of Zeus, though only two can claim Hera as their mother.

The Greeks often referred to these twelve great gods simply as "The Twelve" and worshiped them collectively. Thus you could say that these were the major deities of ancient Greece. But where is Hades—Zeus's other brother and ruler over the realm of the dead? Surely he qualifies as a major deity. Where is Zeus's powerful son Dionysos, who brought dark ecstasies into this sunlit world? And if Aphrodite lives among The Twelve on Olympus, where is her son Eros? Where is Iris? Where is Pan?

Greek Polytheism, like most polytheisms, conceived a very open system of divinity. In place of a clear formal structure, the Greek pantheon showed an organic complexity, involving scores of gods and goddesses of varying origins and overlapping powers. Some gods were honored with temples and festivals; others were not. Some received only local worship; others were known throughout the land.

Most Greeks understood that each deity was related to all the others, but few could have recited a comprehensive genealogy of the gods. Nothing of what a Greek knew about the divine came from dogma. A great deal came from myth.

Family relations among The Twelve, as well as among the whole extended family of gods, gave ancient mythmakers a wealth of lively material. Incidents of divine intervention in human affairs added to their store of subjects. The myths, in turn, gave those who heard them much of their specific knowledge about each deity's nature and deeds. Building on a long oral tradition—with countless accretions and elaborations over several centuries—Greek poets, playwrights, sculptors, and painters continually shaped and reshaped received conceptions of the divine.

Furthermore, the Greek landscape, the seascape, the weather, and many everyday human activities appeared to be infused with holiness. Sacred places abounded, as did sacred moments and sacred situations. In each such place, moment, or situation, one might well discover the presence of a god or a goddess. Opportunities both for encountering and for naming the divine were virtually infinite.

The Greeks found two complementary ways to do the *naming*. Either a deity was unique to a particular location or condition, or that place or condition was merely a particular instance of a more general phenomenon. It's the difference between honoring "Nike," the goddess of victory, as a separate, individualized being, and honoring

"Athena Nike"—the great goddess Athena in her victorious aspect. Similarly, one might pray to "Helios," the sun god, or to "Apollo Helios," a solar Apollo.

The ancients named their gods in both ways, and did so liberally. One result of their tendency toward specificity was the vast array of individual deities. One result of their tendency toward generalization was the selection of The Twelve to stand for and subsume all the rest. We do not know precisely why the Greeks settled on the number twelve, nor why just these twelve were admitted to Olympus. We don't need to discover the origins of such choices, however, to admire their effectiveness.

The number itself is resonant across cultures, from the Twelve Tribes of Israel and the Twelve Apostles of Jesus to the Twelve Nights of Teutonic folklore and the Twelve Knights of the Round Table. Divisible by three and four and six and two, it appeals to our sense of geometric pattern and order.

But the symmetries of The Twelve extend beyond the number. Six gods complement six goddesses, and many of their pairings mirror fundamental relationships among humans, such as brother and sister or man and wife. As I have suggested above, they may also be paired according to their characters or spheres of influence over the affairs of humankind—home and work, land and sea, love and war, and so on.

These "spheres," of course, not only match one another in complementary pairs but also overlap and interpenetrate one another. Taken together, the twelve spheres encompass the whole of human existence. For the Greeks the implication was obvious: everything in human existence partakes of the divine. And the corollary was equally obvious: the human world is an ordered cosmos, mirroring the divine cosmos of Olympus.

This was and remains a sublime vision of ultimate reality. The Twelve are simultaneously beings and ideas. They are simultaneously a flawed family and a perfect number. In their behavior they are virtually human, but in their essences they are entirely other. In them male balances female, nature balances culture, microcosm balances macrocosm, and all the living universe vibrates with a dynamic symmetry.

We speak of The Twelve in the present tense because they are so palpably alive in the present. Like most great works of art, they have outlived the artists who originally formed them. Like most great works of art, they remain open to new interpretations. Like some of the greatest works of art, they continue to shape us and to be shaped by us.

We can find a rough analogy to this in music. A few centuries ago, Antonio Vivaldi composed a set of violin concertos that he called *The Four Seasons*. He put notes down on a page so that an orchestra could read his score and make it audible. Long after Vivaldi's death, the twelve movements of his masterpiece are still performed frequently and remain alive in the ears and minds of modern conductors, players, and listeners.

Think of the poets and artists of ancient Greece as "Vivaldi." Think of their myths, epics, plays, sculptures, paintings, and temples as the notes of his musical score. The twelve gods and goddesses are the music itself. And we who attend to them and continue to shape them are both performers and audience.

Just as the notes that Vivaldi committed to paper enable us to hear the concertos he imagined, so the works of art and literature left to us by the Greeks enable us to see their vividly imagined gods. Just as the music Vivaldi composed can still act upon us in the present, so The Twelve can still affect us directly, informing our feelings, thoughts, and actions in the present. And just as *The Four*

Seasons remain subject to the ever-changing interpretations of today's performers and listeners, so do these gods and goddesses remain subject to our contemporary acts of god-shaping.

We do not disrespect The Twelve by calling them "works of art" or by describing them as "imagined." "Imagined" is not the same as "imaginary;" its opposite is not "real" but "unimagined." All of us apprehend our deities by means of our imaginations.

The Twelve can be as real and as present to us today as are Jesus and Gautama to their followers. They can be as fully conceived and as likely to affect our lives. The details of a historical figure's time on earth do not make that figure any more potent in our present imaginings. Such a factual history may even form an impediment to our seeing the metaphor behind the legend.

On the other hand, the more we learn about a sacred composition, the more prepared we are to appreciate its nuances. Knowing the score, we enjoy the music more.

Σ

FAMILY TRAITS

The Twelve Gods have much in common. They all began as forces of nature. They all vigorously defend their spheres of influence. All of them wield enormous power over humankind. All possess knowledge far broader and deeper than our own. The list is long.

But the god-shapers of ancient Greece found three traits to be essential, central to their idea of divinity: The gods are personal.
The gods are beautiful.
The gods are immortal.

Here the term "personal" means, "having the nature of a person, of a self-conscious being." Most dictionaries follow this definition with its principal application—"a personal god."

The word is useful insofar as some cultures have shaped ideas of the divine or of ultimate reality that are *impersonal*. At one extreme lie pantheism and the Tao and the god of the Stoics, where the divine is too vast, too inclusive, or too abstract to admit of an individuated personality. At the other extreme are the deified forces of nature—god of rain, god of horses—whose characters have not been developed beyond these simple terms of identification.

The Greek gods, by rich contrast, brim with personality. They laugh, they cry, they love, they hate, they are wise, they are foolish, they are lustful, they are chaste, they are obedient and disobedient, selfish and generous. In short, they display nearly every sort of emotion and behavior that we, their human worshipers, display—save fear of disease and death.

Furthermore, these "self-conscious beings" are not merely spirits, but *embodied* persons, differing from one another as we do in height, weight, eye color, muscularity, and in mental and physical skills. They are so much like us, in fact, that sometimes, when they have chosen to walk unheralded among mortals, we have failed to recognize them as gods.

It is the personhood of these gods and goddesses that makes them such good company—divine company—for our human sojourn on this earth. However awesome their power, however perfect their knowledge, we can relate to them as powerful, perfected versions of ourselves.

Equally important, *they* can relate to *us*. The gods could, if they chose, remain aloof on Olympus, occupying a pleasant universe parallel to the one that we inhabit. Instead they interact with us, communicate with us, guide us, and respond to our prayers. Occasionally this interaction achieves an intimacy unknown to most religions: a god makes love to a mortal woman, a goddess to a mortal man.

According to legend, the most frequent cause for such an extraordinary union has been the attraction of the god or goddess to the physical beauty of that particular human being. The mortal exhibits such a god-like—that is, beautiful—appearance that the barrier between divine and human momentarily disappears.

It would be fair to say that the ancient Greeks were obsessed with beauty. Alert to the full range of sensuous beauties they saw in the world around them, they also revered the *idea* of beauty. Philosophers discussed it as an ultimate good; poets and playwrights sang its praises; painters and potters, sculptors and architects sought to achieve it in their creations.

Judging from the physical remnants of Greek civilization that we can still see today—temples, vases, statues, mosaics—the artists' efforts met with extraordinary success. More than two thousand five hundred years after its creation, the majestic perfection of the Parthenon still stuns contemporary visitors. Despite the long centuries of shifting taste, today's museumgoers still pause in wonder and pleasure before a gracefully formed clay cup or a delightfully naturalistic bronze animal.

No more beautiful Greek objects remain for our admiration and contemplation than the images of their gods. Sculpted in marble or bronze, varying in size from the length of a finger to greater than human scale, these sacred statues now populate hundreds of museums (and private collections) throughout the world. Such images allow us to glimpse something of what the Greeks saw when confronting their deities.

These statues seem thoroughly human. They stand or stride or sit or kneel like us. Often they are naked or only lightly robed. No halos crown their heads. No rays of light stream from their bodies. Some figures are accompanied by attributes—a bow for Artemis, a trident for Poseidon—but most are not. How do we know they are gods? Because they are serenely self-contained. Because they are ideally proportioned. Because they are without blemish. Because they are so beautiful.

Only a small step separates the beauty of some favored humans from that of the gods. Likewise, the gap between our personhood and divine personhood is only a matter of degree. But in regard to the third essential feature of the gods—their immortality—a chasm yawns between them and us. They live forever. We die.

Among the ancient Greeks the most common term for "human being" was "mortal," just as the most common term for "divine being" was "immortal." While fully cognizant of all the ways in which gods and humans differ, the Greeks found the defining distinction to be that one species dies, the other doesn't.

It is a distinction, of course, that makes a huge difference in how the members of each species may properly live their lives. The gods need no clocks. What is not done today may be put off until tomorrow or indeed until the next millennium. By contrast, we race against time, and every breath brings us closer to death. The gods may suffer loss or disappointment or even physical pain, but they have an eternity in which to get over it. For us, suffering may last a lifetime, and mistakes may be fatal.

This puts a strain upon the empathy discussed above. In this matter the gods do not hold our hands or offer words of comfort. Instead they frequently go out of their way to emphasize the disparity between us. Apollo's dictum, "Know yourself," is first and foremost a reminder of our mortality. If such reminders are not gentle, they are certainly apt. We are being admonished to get on with it in this life because we have no other and the clock is ticking.

By being immortal, the gods get us off the hook. Eternal life is what *they* do. It is no business of ours.

T

STANDING OUTSIDE

Twelve major gods. Three essential traits. It all seems so very neat and tidy. If my description has made Greek Polytheism look like a closed, well-organized system, the fault is entirely mine.

In truth, the religious ideas and practices of the ancient Greeks defy modern attempts at codification. Heavy tomes have been written describing important features, finding significant patterns. They do not pretend to exhaust their subject. Even weightier books try to comprehend the myriad interconnected and richly mutable Greek myths.

The Greeks themselves—who invented so much— did not invent systematic theology, and they produced no Thomas Aquinas capable of tying all this complexity up with a bow. Their shaping of divinity lay chiefly in the hands of poets not priests. Therefore it remained in flux, yielding a proliferation of deities, symbols, rituals, festivals, temples, shrines...all of which were subject to continual shifts in meaning and changes in relative importance.

Even membership in The Twelve occasionally came up for grabs. A new god or goddess might prove so powerful, so essential to the Greeks' view of the world that he or she might legitimately demand inclusion among the Olympians. Such a god is Dionysos, a most untidy deity.

He is the tardy guest at the feast—tipsy, loud, and of questionable pedigree. (Unlike the other gods, he had one human parent.) Yet he turns out to be a welcome addition and the life of the party. His presence allows the other guests to forget themselves in revelry.

Dionysos is god of the grapevine and of the wine produced from the grape and of the intoxication produced by the wine. The Greeks saw these things intertwined and honored the god who was present in all three.

Though he rose to prominence somewhat later than the other major deities, his worship quickly became an integral part of Greek culture. He enhanced the festivals of the other gods, while his own festivals celebrated festivity itself. Two widely divergent but complementary elements coexisted in the feasts of Dionysos—first an ecstatic strain, encouraging a kind of exalted madness; and second a theatrical strain, which eventually developed into classical tragedy and comedy.

Both strains involved masks and role-playing. In the first case, worshipers abandoned their ordinary behavior and ordinary clothing, left human habitation for the wild countryside at night, put on masks, lost themselves in frenzied celebration, and identified (every one of them) with the god himself. In the second case, a far more controlled celebration took place by day, in town, within a well-defined sacred space. Only a small number of trained actors and dancers wore the masks and embodied the roles required by each play. Still, the others present participated fully, more a congregation than an audience.

Greeks were masters at finding the general principle within diverse particulars. Despite our great remove in time, we can easily detect the common theme in their worship of Dionysos.

When a man is observed to be inebriated, whether he's a happy drunk or a sad one, we say he's "not himself." The stage actor dons a mask and takes on the persona of someone other than himself. The god-intoxicated worshiper loses himself in ecstasy. The Greek word *ekstasis*, "standing outside," applies in a metaphorical sense to all three states.

Dionysos is the patron of who we are when we are not ourselves. No wonder he captured the allegiance of the Greeks. Imagine that your world is an ordered cosmos, presided over—or at least watched over—by the gods. Every conscious human thought, every deliberate human act gains value from this fact. Even your passionate desires fall within this cosmos, even your bursts of rage in the heat of battle.

But what about your unbidden thoughts? Your unintended acts? Your unconscious moments? Your ecstasies? Whether drink or drama or religious fervor is the cause, where are The Twelve when you stand outside yourself? Are they not absent? Be of good cheer: Dionysos is here.

And he remains as crucial for us today as he was for the Greeks. Being human is still a full-time job. The gods encourage us to live our lives intensely, meaningfully. They remind us of what we can achieve when we are most ourselves. But occasionally we fall short of their challenge, escaping into alcohol, drugs, or mindless inattention. Sometimes, though fully conscious, we watch a movie or a TV drama and lose ourselves in the narratives of others. More rarely, and only momentarily, we may transcend our normal lives, rising in imagination to a mystic state beyond identification with a separate self.

These states of mind, or states of being, may seem as different from one another as air, earth, and water. Even so, we can understand how they share a single realm and contribute to a common reality. Picture a vineyard, where sun-warmed air, fertile earth, and nourishing rain combine to bring the grapes to ripeness. The means are many; the end is one.

Whenever, however we manage to escape from ourselves, we remain in divine company. Our excursions outside the familiar self need not be feared or merely tolerated. We may *celebrate* them as Dionysos's gift.

Υ

AFTER LIFE

Modern archaeologists exploring the cemeteries of ancient Athens unearthed some of the most moving images in the history of art. Above each grave stood a stone slab with a single scene carved on its face. The scene showed the deceased alone or in the company of family or friends. All were presented as in life.

A soldier appears in new armor. A child holds her pet. A young woman gives a jewelry box to an older woman. A husband tenderly clasps the hand of his wife. The poignancy of these images lies in their dignified depiction of heartbreaking loss. The figures show their sorrow by a downcast gaze, a resigned posture. The mood is neither hysteria nor hope. It is human grief, restrained but profound. The person mourned is not shown dead, or dying. We see the soldier whole, before the battle. We see the wife healthy, before childbirth. The focus is on the richness of the life left behind.

Of an afterlife we see nothing at all. For these Athenians, what occurred after death was scarcely worthy of representation. A person's spirit descended to the dark underworld, where it remained—bodiless, voiceless, and powerless—a shadow of the former self. The spirit had nothing more to fear but also nothing to hope for. Achilles, hero of the *Iliad*, spoke for most Greeks when he said he'd rather be a poor man's slave on earth than a king among the dead.

In any case, the dead already had their king, and he was not a hero but a god. Hades, brother to Zeus and Poseidon, ruled the underworld as his brothers ruled the sky and the sea.

The dead were in good hands, for Hades was known to be just. Socrates in the *Phaedo* calls him "a good and prudent god." Yet the living did not worship him as they worshiped The Twelve. They preferred not to rush things.

Hades was "the unseen." He seldom left his realm beneath the earth, and when he did, he chose to remain invisible. He was also called "the rich one" or "the generous," source of all the organic and mineral wealth that grew up, or was brought up from below.

An important myth recounts how Hades secretly abducted lovely Persephone, daughter of the great goddess Demeter, and carried her down to the underworld to be his wife. When she learned of this, Demeter refused to let any vegetation grow on earth until her daughter was restored to the world of the living. Eventually Zeus resolved the impasse with a compromise: Persephone could return to the sunlit world for two-thirds of every year; the other third she would spend with Hades.

This story (in its original, more vivid and more complex form) carried a host of meanings for the ancient Greeks. Chief among them was the conjoining of death and regeneration. The myth links the god of death with the goddess of vegetal growth by means of a wife/daughter who moves perpetually between them.

Later Greek epitaphs make this link explicit: "May your bones bloom into violets and lilies, May you blossom in rose-petals...So that generations to come shall have a flower from you."

In their shaping of Hades, the Greeks repeatedly answered the radical discontinuity of death with affirmations of continuity. Dying, we depart from the bright world but not from the company of the gods. The god who greets us has been, while we lived, an unseen source of our prosperity. By going to him we participate in the universal cycle of decay and regeneration.

Such continuities provide an attractive framework for thinking about death in the abstract. But when we suffer the loss of someone we love, or face the certainty of our own death, these ideas offer at best only partial consolation. In the presence of a *particular* death, the ancient Greeks consoled one another in much the same way as we do today, expressing sympathy to the bereaved, endorsing and sharing their grief. They spoke of the inevitability of death and of its welcome release from pain and suffering. They said that the deceased had only been "lent" to the living, and that time would eventually heal their sorrow.

The mourners' chief consolation lay in recounting specific memories of the particular life that had been lived. There was praise for the cherished individual, for his or her relationships, deeds, and accomplishments. There was assurance that he or she would live on in memory, the only sort of immortality to which mortals could aspire.

Of course, neither the continuities of Hades nor the consolations of memory allowed Greeks to ignore the central fact—human beings die. Our ability to see and hear and smell and taste the inexpressible beauty of this world ceases. Our experience of a conscious mind carried in a working body ceases. Our chance to embrace one another, warmth to human warmth, ceases.

Rather than flinching before the fact of death, the Greeks found it to be the ultimate reason for squeezing the most from every moment. Their response to death cries out across three millennia: Live now! Live well! Live purposefully! Live honorably! Live!

Yet even in the great age of Greece, there were some who wanted more. Many were drawn to the mystery religions, which existed side by side with worship of The Twelve but offered their initiates hope of a better future. Plato and other deep thinkers developed theories about the immortality of the soul. In the popular imagination, Elysium, a paradise once reserved for only the greatest heroes, became a plausible destination for anyone who had lived an exemplary life.

During the ensuing centuries—as Greece fell under the sway first of Macedonia, then of Rome—the idea that human beings might somehow survive death gained credibility. Throughout the Mediterranean a host of religions, old and new, offered competing visions of an afterlife.

Most successful of these was Christianity, which combined its narrative of a suffering, dying, buried, and resurrected god with a potent message for the "pagan" world: "Christ has abolished death and brought life everlasting." Those who believed could anticipate not only personal immortality but also bodily resurrection.

Here was consolation worthy of the name. "Good news," indeed! Converts multiplied, apparently untroubled by the seismic shift in religious focus from this life to the next.

An eminent classical historian once wrote: "To educated Greeks, Christianity was to appear as a religion of the grave." But within the vast empire ruled from Rome, most people were neither educated nor Greek.

ONE ANSWER

"The triumph of monotheism" is a good story with a bad premise: Worship of a single god constitutes an advance, a spiritual improvement over worship of many gods and goddesses. For over fifteen hundred years, monotheism has defined religion for the West and monotheists have taught us their version of religious progress.

Most of us begin to learn this prejudice at the moment we first encounter polytheism. We read or are told that worship of a plural divine was a necessary but primitive stage in human spiritual development. It has now—with the arrival of Yahweh or Allah or Whomever—been surpassed and superseded.

Of course it was not "monotheism" *per se* that captured the religious imagination of the Roman Empire (and thus of Europe). It was Christianity. Few Greek or Roman polytheists, attracted to a superior theology, had been rushing to convert to Judaism.   But one tiny Jewish sect—energized by Paul of Tarsus, whose god-shaping skills were second to none—went after converts with extraordinary zeal. Christianity had a lot to offer besides monotheism: a compelling legend, a resurrected Savior, a novel moral code, "redemption from sin," and best of all, eternal life.

Unfortunately by mixing a claim to universality with a rigid dogmatism, it also offered a recipe for intolerance. We all know the sad historical result. In less than one century Rome moved from tolerating Christianity, to making it the state religion, to banning all "pagan" forms of worship.

While consolidating their position, the Fathers of the early Church took great pains to discredit the beliefs, rituals, and mores of their "pagan" contemporaries. But the polytheism that had once been vigorous enough to pose a threat was later dismissed as no more than a footnote to the main thrust of religious history—that is, an inexorable ascent toward acknowledging the One True God.

The idea that one god is better than many is so widely shared in our culture—even by our atheists —that defending it hardly seems necessary. If pressed, an intelligent believer might point to monotheism's innate appeal to an intellect seeking clarity and integration. One god implies a unified spiritual universe, and if he be a creator-god, one creator. Moreover, the psychological advantage should be obvious: the consolation of a single answer to a multitude of spiritual questions.

Monotheism's assumptions about its inherent superiority may not, however, withstand scrutiny from "outside the box." Consider its notion of progress—a strong religious idea inevitably supplants a weaker one. The history of Christianity itself subverts this view.

Despite the carefully turned phrases of its early creeds, Christianity was blessed from the start with a built-in tendency toward polytheism. Look at the doctrine of the Trinity—"one God in three persons"—established by the early Christian Church.

In John's Gospel we find Jesus telling his followers, "I will pray to the Father, and he will give you another Comforter, who will abide with you forever." Inspired by this same Comforter (the Holy Spirit), the early disciples preached the good news taught by Jesus (the only Son of God), that the Kingdom of God (the Father Almighty) was at hand. Now does anyone without a degree in theology see a *single* divine being here, rather than three? If so, let us call the ancient Greek religion "monotheism" as well, and talk about "one god in twelve persons."

By the High Middle Ages in Europe, authentic "pagans" were thin on the ground (not by accident) yet Christianity continued to tend the flame of polytheism. The Catholic Church readily sponsored the veneration of the "Mother of God" along with a rich proliferation of holy saints in heaven, each with the power to effect miracles and to intercede with the Supreme Being. Popes and churchmen tried to hold the monotheistic line, claiming a fundamental theological distinction between their singular (that is, "triune") God and his host of sainted subordinates. But certainly no time-traveler from ancient Greece would have been fooled. Here was Zeus again and his family of subordinate deities. The Church had reverted to the ancient European norm of a plural divine.

This polytheistic tendency in Roman Catholicism has remained vigorous to this day and beyond the confines of Europe. Witness the syncretic beliefs and practices of the modern Catholic faithful in Africa and the Americas, where many confessing Christians regularly acknowledge a multitude of supernatural beings.

If the contention that one god inevitably supersedes many gods cannot be supported by history, common sense can tell us why. The monotheistic God suffers the burden of being singular in a world that is manifestly plural. And for all the protestations of theologians that He is, by definition, "limitless," His very singularity limits Him.

The infamous "problem of evil" illustrates this: If God is all-good, all-knowing, and all-powerful, how can evil exist? Only recently have some monotheists begun to deal with the issue by saying, "Well, maybe He's just a little bit bad (or ignorant, or impotent)."

Believers have devised a number of other strategies to cope with their experience of a God Who is supposed to be a loving Father but Who allows some of His children to perpetrate heinous evil and others to suffer unbearable harm. One strategy is to say, "It may look like evil now, but God knows it's for our ultimate good." Another is to say that what we humans perceive as evil, namely human suffering and human wickedness, God sees differently. The ultimate strategy is to acknowledge that God's ways are unfathomable to mere mortals. Who are we to comprehend the will of the Creator and Sustainer of the Universe, let alone to question it? But you will note that the comfort of a single God providing a single answer to all our spiritual questions loses some of its appeal if the single answer is: "Don't ask."

The singularity of the One God limits Him in other ways as well. Students of literature have long remarked that God as a dramatic character cannot hold a candle to Satan—not because goodness and omnipotence are dull ideas in themselves, but because a being who is thoroughly good and thoroughly powerful is without inflection. He is less interesting than most of His creatures (Satan included) because he is less nuanced.

Fortunately for monotheism, one of its characteristic claims about the One True God— that He is unchanging—has been proven false by generations of creative god-shapers. We can follow the history of Yahweh, for example, through three thousand years of significant changes: from a warlike tribal god in ancient Israel; to a Heavenly Father concerned with the salvation of all peoples in the early Roman

Empire; to a much-less-gendered and much-more-amorphous Ground of Being in the recent past.

The god-shapers of monotheism seem to be engaged in an endless tug-of-war between those who would fix their Deity now and for all time, and those who respond to changes in the human sphere by shaping changes in heaven. The dogmas created by the former group continually impede the accommodations made by the latter, and vice versa. This creative tension serves at least to keep the One God alive in milieus that otherwise would have passed Him by. But the downside is severe. In a community that defines itself by what it believes, coherent and convincing belief remains an ever-elusive goal for the educated faithful.

Polytheism, of course, enjoys some creative tensions of its own, as competing visions of the divine jostle for the imaginations of worshipers. Here, however, a variety of views can hardly be called a *problem*, since all may serve to enrich our understanding of Olympus.

We have to admire the determination of monotheists who are still spiritually alive, and are willing to work like water against granite for their cause. Let them go on trying to shape their

One God for His third millennium. We wish them luck—and patience. But we must ask them to remember, in their zeal, not to confuse a good story with the whole story.

X

MULTIPLE CHOICE

We are all human. We are all god-shapers. Yet some of us tend to be more active in our shaping. We take religious questions seriously and search for serious answers, but seldom do we discover them "inside the box" or in any organized religion. Our own religion is a work in progress. We are always on the road, never at home.

We "seekers" may feel a twinge of envy for people who seem content in the faith of their parents, or for those who have broken free of one religion only to find a secure home in another. Many of us may harbor a desire to end our seeking and actually find.

Nevertheless, we represent a category of religious experience far more positive and fruitful than "none of the above." For us human consciousness is an ever-present wonder and the divine an ever-present mystery. We may, on occasion, sense something vast and awesome nearby without knowing for certain whether it is a mountain or an abyss. As seekers, we tend to move *toward* this unknown thing, equally ready to climb or to plunge.

Presented with a new religious idea—or an old one that may be new to us—we seekers are prepared to give it a fair hearing. Usually we glean from it what we can, and then go on with our search. What can we glean from Greek Polytheism?

Most obviously, this religion invites us to see the divine as plural rather than as singular. What's more, it helps us rethink the very concept of "religion," leaving out features we thought were essential and putting in features we thought were a-religious or anti-religious. Greek Polytheism really *is* different.

But one must immediately ask: Is it any more appropriate for us than the religions we have rejected? Or more appealing than the many other forms of spirituality currently on offer in our culture? Do we find anything here that could turn a contemporary seeker into a worshiper of The Twelve?

Clearly this ancient religion has not lost its relevance. We have already noted several of its certifiably "modern" concerns—with nature, with inclusiveness, with sexuality, with technology, and so on. But four core elements combine, I believe, to make this Olympian religion particularly suitable for the present day.

First, it relies on metaphor as its principal route to meaning, permitting a much more flexible and nuanced approach to divine matters than one often finds elsewhere. A preference for metaphor also means that the insights of this religion will always remain compatible with those of science.

Second, Greek Polytheism is grounded in a great historical reality—the culture that shaped it and was in turn shaped by it. Anyone choosing to embrace these deities today joins a famously productive religious tradition, which has proven beneficial not only to individual worshipers but also to their society.

Third, Greek Polytheism assumes that both its deities and their worshipers will continue to evolve, shaped—on the human side—chiefly by the arts and literature. Therefore the religion cannot become static (or iconoclastic, which may be worse), and it positively *requires* human creativity in order to sustain itself.

Fourth, this religion encourages an expansive view of the world and of humanity in the world. Every human experience, thought, and action falls within the purview of one deity or another. The divine is always within reach, cleansing the doors of human perception so that everything may appear as it really is: holy.

Taken separately, not one of these four core elements is especially modern. Taken together, however, they signify an approach uniquely matched to the spiritual needs of our time.

When Marx called religion "the opiate of the people," he slighted this Olympian religion which has always been a *stimulant*. Their gods drew the Greeks into a highly energized world, suffused with meaning and charged with purpose. The same energy, meaning, and purpose are available to us today insofar as we choose to engage the same deities.

There is no question that we *can* engage them if we make the effort. We already possess the classic means for approaching the divine: sacred symbols and images. Greek poets, painters, and sculptors left us a cornucopia of such things.

We may learn the individual attributes of each god and goddess lightning, lyre, bow, trident, torch.... Then we will find a host of associations with particular plants and animals: Zeus's oak, Athena's olive, Apollo's laurel, the peacocks of Hera, the sheep of Hermes, the deer of Artemis.... Even the sun, the moon, the land, and the sea may serve as symbols for particular deities.

The symbolic net of this religion is cast so wide, in fact, that the more myths we know and the more signs we recognize, the more divine connections we are likely to discover.

The Greeks have also given us countless images of the gods and goddesses themselves and plenty of verbal cues to supplement all the visual ones. Brief epithets capture some telling aspect of an individual deity's nature. Tales from myth and legend expand our knowledge of his or her character and deeds.

Learning such things may take some work on our part, but it should be worth the effort. Because everything we learn about the gods brings us closer to knowing them. The Greeks seldom spoke of "faith" or of "believing in" their deities.

They used the expression "to know the gods," affirming both the existence of a transcendent realm and the human ability to comprehend it.

This "knowing" demands neither a direct encounter nor any sort of special event. It requires a special state of mind. The deity is fully present to one's imagination and an active agent within it. Knowing the gods allows us to be, to think, and to act in relation to them. And this very interaction helps us know them better.

A contemporary seeker who came this far—learning the symbols, reading the myths, knowing the gods—would have reached the threshold of a living religion (and left "Mythology 101" behind). But how would he or she actually practice such a religion?

We know what the Greeks did. They worshiped the gods with prayers, hymns, dances, sacrifices, libations, and processions. Often they gave their "first fruits" to The Twelve. They built altars, shrines, and temples for them. They organized annual festivals and sacred contests in their honor.

When an entire culture joins in worship, we would expect no less. But the modern seeker is a lone individual in a non-Greek world. And this ancient religion is virtually new to us. If we wish to engage these gods in the present, we will have to improvise.

Perhaps the most natural response to a known and accessible deity is prayer. The Greeks offered their gods praise, asked them for aid, and gave them thanks. We could surely do the same. Nationwide festivals may not be available to us but private rituals certainly are. One can imagine a personal shrine, a family feast, or an occasional libation for the gods.

Imagination will be key here, because the seeker will have taken his or her god-shaping to an entirely new level. Gleaning may be one thing; worshiping is another. If the skeptic in you asks, "Is it worth the trouble?" the skeptic in me answers, "Try it and see."

Allow me to offer an example of one seeker's improvisation: Not far from my home there is a wooded hillside above a stream. In a flat clearing surrounded by oaks stand twelve large stones—an outer ring of eight; then three in the center supporting a thick triangular slab. This stone circle was set up just fifteen years ago by a local band of neo-pagans. But I have come to identify each of its stones with one of The Twelve.

Once a day throughout the year I walk to the clearing and pay my respects to the gods. In a simple ritual I visit each of the stones in turn, walking counter-clockwise inside the outer ring: Hestia, Hephaistos, Demeter, Poseidon, Aphrodite, Ares, Athena, Hermes; and then clockwise outside the inner ring: Artemis, Apollo, Hera; concluding with Zeus (the triangular stone). Pausing before each stone, I place my hand on it and say a prayer of thanks to the god or goddess for his or her particular gifts.

Sometimes I make a request. I have asked Hermes to bring my wife home safely from a trip to India. I have asked Artemis to grant my grandmother a good death. I have asked Apollo to ease the pain of a close friend. I have asked Athena for help with my research. In all of these cases the gods have been kind.

Perhaps their greatest kindness has been the stone circle itself. Though not my invention, it offers me a series of symbols, a setting for ritual, and a focus for prayer. The stones are at once icons and architecture. The inner four form an altar; the outer eight serve as boundary stones, defining the sacred precinct.

The Greeks called a sacred precinct a *temenos*, and marked its boundary with stones or a wall. The *temenos* was holy ground. It might be dedicated to a single deity or to many. It might hold several temples or none at all. Always it encompassed an altar.

Such *temene* dotted the landscape of ancient Greece, along with innumerable smaller shrines. Over the course of centuries, the gods had made their presence known so widely that places sacred to them could be found everywhere.

What stood outside the *temenos*? If the Greeks confronted the sacred at every turn, where did they confront the profane? Their language had four words for "sacred," one of which meant, in part, "not sacred in that other way." And their word for "profane" often meant simply "outside the sacred." The divine penetrated every facet of their daily lives. They could move into the realm of the profane only by turning away from their deities.

Nearly two millennia separate us from those Greeks, and most of us inhabit a landscape devoid of *temene*, temples, and shrines. But right here, right now, we can enjoy the company of the gods. They will be as vivid to us and as present in our lives as we permit them to be. When we attend to them fully, the sacred will again be the rule; the profane, again the exception.

Whether we modern seekers choose to adopt this religion *as* a religion or prefer just to take from it what we can, Greek Polytheism tells us that we need no longer seek a religious home. We are already there. The *temenos* of the gods embraces all the earth. We are searching on holy ground.

Ψ

SHAPING US

Although many believe that the British Museum should return its fine collection of Parthenon sculptures to Greece, a director of the National Museum in Athens has spoken against it. So long as the Parthenon Frieze is displayed in London, he argued, and the Aphrodite of Melos is seen in Paris, and the Pergamon Altar in Berlin, and the Laocoön Group in Rome, "we are all Greeks."

This position is both generous and smart. It finesses the vexed questions of who sold what to whom when and for how much. By refusing to demand the repatriation of major ancient works, it reaffirms that those works transcend their ethnicity. They belong to the world, and thus the world belongs to them.

Because we receive our legacy from ancient Greece through such public means—statues, buildings, books, and plays—rather than through family genealogies or private rituals, we see this legacy as universal rather than tribal. Those of us without a drop of Greek blood, without a word of the language, may take as much pride in "our Greek heritage" as any contemporary Greek.

But the fact is we are not *ancient* Greeks, nor would most of us wish to be. Few women would envy their ancient counterparts, who received no formal education and enjoyed neither political nor economic equality with men. Similarly, no one living today would wish to have been a slave in Greece, even if slavery came from losing a war or from going into debt and wasn't a question of race. We may not even wish to trade places with a prosperous male citizen—the top of the social pyramid—considering his financial obligations to the *polis*, his frequent military duties, his short life span, and his chances of finding a good dentist.

Slavery and gender inequity, the most serious flaws in their society from our perspective, did not originate with the Greeks. Both were customary in the ancient world, and we can fault Greek civilization only for failing to abolish them. Nevertheless, they serve to remind us that the goal of our god-shaping cannot be a recreation of the past.

Ancient Greece had its moment in history. That moment may have been magnificent but it has passed. What has not passed is our rich legacy from Greek civilization, the objects and ideas we may still look at and think about.

A great classicist called the gods and goddesses of the Greeks "their best ideas." While each of these ideas was shaped in a very specific time and place, they now transcend that time and place, like the artifacts discussed earlier. We can enjoy the beauty and power of the Parthenon sculptures only in the present. We can know the power and beauty of the gods only in the present.

In an earlier chapter we examined the immortals' profound effect upon the society that shaped them. But now it is a new age and a new game. The gods' effect on us, if we choose to take them seriously, will surely be something new.

What might that effect be? What might the gods ask of us? The following precepts are no more than a series of educated guesses, based on what we know about The Twelve and what we know about ourselves.

1) Respect Nature. For us, as for the gods, nature is the primary context. We come from it, live in it, and eventually return to it. We must honor the earth as if she were our mother, our home, our sustenance, and our inspiration, for she is all of these and more. This requires action in the real world, where conserving fossil fuels, recycling waste, reforesting, and restoring clean air and water must become our sacred duties.

2) Respect Humanity. We are the *nearly* godlike species, "human company" to the gods, and capable like them of understanding and changing the world. All equally mortal, we share a common status in the eyes of The Twelve, so that our lapses into inequality are an affront to them. Inequality based on gender, for example, is incompatible with the gender balance on Olympus. And for one of us to dominate another, or even to govern another without his or her consent, mocks the dominion of the gods.

3) Respect Unity and Diversity. Multiple spheres of influence are joined in one divine family. We continually experience the world's multiplicity and continually look for its unifying patterns. Because our world is plural, our lives are full of surprises. Because our world is singular, we can sometimes see it whole. The Twelve, in their diversity, ask us to respect the infinite variety of

the particulars we encounter—in nature, in human beings, in ideas. The Twelve, in their unity, ask us to respect the ordered Cosmos. We need not choose between these poles.

4) Value Tolerance. A tendency toward openness and inclusiveness is a fundamental feature of Greek Polytheism. If their human worshipers require it, the gods stand ready to welcome a new god or goddess to Olympus. Such openness provides a model for us. We should not only practice religious tolerance but also tolerate our human differences of every sort, whether they arise from accidents of birth, or from accidents of acculturation, or from deliberate choices.

5) Value Education. Each of The Twelve has taught humanity something practical or theoretical or moral. They expect us to continue learning, though we must learn most things on our own. Part of our education will be pursued entirely for its own sake, because the world is simply too interesting to ignore. Part of our education will yield immediate and concrete results. And part of our education will bring us closer to the will of the gods. In this Olympian religion, knowledge always precedes wisdom.

6) Value Excellence and Balance. The gods place these two very different goals before us, expecting

every human to strive for both at once. Far from being incompatible, the two temper each other's excesses. The world's smartest physicist needs to remember she has a body. The world's strongest weight-lifter needs to remember he has a brain. Yet none of us should be so committed to a life of moderation that we never make the effort to excel.

7) Act Ethically. Each of us faces the challenge of learning to distinguish good from bad and right from wrong. Then, having identified them, we must choose the right and the good. Easier said than done! The gods require us to act honorably, and they have given us some signposts for moral behavior, but they have not provided a complete map. We are left to discover for ourselves how to interact properly with nature and with each other, applying our reason, intuition, and experience.

8) Act Reasonably. The human faculty of reason is one of our most godlike traits, and The Twelve clearly respect it in us. With their respect, however, comes an expectation that we will behave according to reason's dictates. In our everyday lives, this just means acting sensibly. When we confront more complex issues, it means applying reason as a necessary—and often controlling—strategy both for understanding and for action.

9) Act Creatively. The gods of Olympus love the arts. Creative themselves, they admire creativity in us, and frequently they inspire it. For three thousand years many of our finest works of art have owed their existence directly or indirectly to The Twelve. The gods are also inventors and innovators in fields far removed from the arts. We can anticipate divine support for all kinds of human innovation.

10) Enjoy Beauty. These beautiful goddesses and gods place beauty in a class by itself among the good things of our world. We seldom confront the divine beings in their full personhood and we also cannot aspire to their immortality. Beauty is the common ground between them and us, our primary means of connection. Every time we see a beautiful view, hear a beautiful sound, or touch a beautiful object, we come closer to the divine.

11) Enjoy Your Body. The gods are *embodied* persons, alert to the sensuous possibilities of life in a physical body. They remind us to appreciate everything we can see, hear, smell, taste, and touch in this world. Most especially, they encourage us to enjoy our sexuality (as most of them enjoy theirs). Because we are human, we need not make love solely to make babies. The gods tell us to desire, and to connect, and to bring

one another pleasure, wholly for the sensual delight involved in these acts.

12) Enjoy the Moment. A leading religious scholar of the last century caught the essence of the Olympian religion: "It reveals the bliss of existing, of sharing in the spontaneity of life and the majesty of the world. The surest way to escape from time is to exploit the wealth of the lived instant." The gods can expect an eternity of these lived instants, while we can count on relatively few of them. So come, let us celebrate the bliss of existing.

Not one of these principles is carved in stone. Each should be read as an invitation rather than as a commandment. While we have identified twelve such invitations, there may well be more. Taken together, they imply a ringing endorsement of the physical world and of our human place within it. This is just what we would expect from gods who look so much like us and who are children of the same mother. Greek Polytheism is surely one of the most humanistic religions the world has known.

Naturally there is no talk of sin, repentance, or redemption in these "pagan" precepts. Christians may be more surprised that there is no explicit mandate to feed the hungry or to comfort the sick.

134

Neither charity nor compassion is proclaimed as a specifically *religious* duty; both are welcome expressions of the ethical behavior prescribed above. The gods—having taught us the healing arts, having encouraged us to connect with one another and to respect our humanity—expect human beings to cope with human suffering. Our mortal ills are not of special concern to them unless we ask directly for their help.

What *is* of special concern to them? Our level of engagement with the phenomenal world. Repeatedly the gods urge us to look outward: to nature, to our society, to other individuals. If the Olympian religion seems strange to most Christians, it must seem equally so to most Buddhists. Instead of giving us a path toward non-attachment and liberation from suffering, The Twelve ask us to feel both our joys and our sorrows intensely, to own them, and to respond to them as if they really matter.

Ideas have consequences. Religious ideas affect how we think about things other than religion, and affect how we act as well. Should we worship one deity or many? Should we focus on this life or on an afterlife? Is the divine a matter of fact or a matter of metaphor? Are truths to be found in myth or in scripture? Our answers to these questions mold our lives.

When a religion publishes a set of guiding principles, even an outsider can glimpse some of the consequences of following that religion. The first noble truth of Buddhism is: "All life is suffering." The first commandment of Judaism and Christianity is: "You will have no other gods before me." The first invitation of the Olympian religion is: "Respect nature." In each case, many of the later precepts flow from the initial one. And in each case, priorities are clear.

What are your priorities? Do you wish to be shaped in the way the Olympian gods would shape you? If so, you need only pay more attention to them. Notice their presence. Listen to what they tell you.

Ω

SHAPING UP

The gods and goddesses of ancient Greece, being immortal, did not die with the society that shaped them. They have lived on—both in themselves, as essential beings, and as inspirations for artists and poets and thinkers of the last two millennia.

During some periods, such as the Middle Ages, we mortals have nearly lost sight of them. During others, such as the Renaissance, we have seen them with much of their original radiance. During this period, in our time, we have an opportunity to encounter them anew.

In the last two chapters we tried to imagine how these gods and goddesses might transform our individual lives. Without doubt, their effect on each one of us could be profoundly liberating and stimulating. But the Greek example also suggests a larger possibility. These gods could radically transform our whole culture.

What if a modern society came to "know the gods" collectively, just as all of Greece once knew them? Surely these gods would enliven that society, as they once enlivened the Greeks. Surely they would move it toward engagement and achievement.

But one can imagine a still more exciting possibility, a divine gift to the entire human race. These gods could provide the catalyst we need to draw our species out of its extended adolescence.

In our infancy, we humans discovered the forms of the world, and discovered ourselves as one distinct form among many. In our childhood, we learned language; then used it to name the forms and to toy with them. The onset of puberty, thrilling and terrible, occurred about five thousand years ago. Our hormones raged; our context expanded; our toys became tools with which we reshaped every form in sight.

Simultaneously we sought to understand other, less visible forms—behind, or above, or beneath the visible world. During this age, experience and intuition were too often turned into "belief." And as quickly, our form-shaping tools were too often turned into form-destroying weapons.

Empires have risen and fallen, cultures have grown and decayed, but humanity hasn't budged from this developmental stage. Perhaps these wise and nearly human gods, by inviting us to re-imagine ourselves, could help us move on to the *next* stage.

This is not a question of our personal maturity. Individual human beings of every era and culture have managed to mature (or not) within the parameters of their era and culture. For all we know, there may have been some highly evolved Huns or Vandals. Conversely, we can be certain there were many childish Greeks.

But when we consider our collective maturation, neither Western civilization nor human beings in general can be said to have come very far in five thousand years. Yes, we have multiplied prodigiously. We have built and destroyed prodigiously. But ethically, morally, and spiritually we are still running in place.

Religions have frequently reminded us of our inadequacies, and told us firmly what we could not or should not do. What if our religion urged us to experiment and to embrace complexity and paradox? What if our religion urged us to think, to act, to create, and to enjoy life, as though everything we did were a celebration of our humanity? What if our religion urged us to treat the whole planet as holy ground?

The human species has always had its prodigies. One infant points to the sky and says "moon" before the others can say "mama." One child learns music while his playmates bang on pans. One adolescent ponders the nature of time while his contemporaries compare designer watches.

Thanks to their gods, the Greeks were the precocious adolescents of the human race. Three thousand years after their youthful fire first illuminated the world, we can still catch a spark.

Perhaps as a culture and as a species, we may not yet aspire to full maturity. But how welcome, how very splendid it would be for us to cross over into adulthood.

The Greeks have bequeathed us personal, beautiful, immortal companions for our journey. Are we ready to begin?